Giza Occasional Papers 4

Giza Plateau Mapping Project
Season 2008
Preliminary Report

Giza Occasional Papers 4

Giza Plateau Mapping Project
Season 2008
Preliminary Report

Mark Lehner, Mohsen Kamel, and Ana Tavares

with contributions by Mary Anne Murray, Jessica Kaiser, Yukinori Kawae, Kosuke Sato, Hiroyuki Kamei, Tomoaki Nakano, and Ichiroh Kanaya

SERIES EDITORS

Wilma Wetterstrom
and
Alexandra Witsell

Ancient Egypt Research Associates, Inc.

Published by Ancient Egypt Research Associates, Inc.
26 Lincoln Street, Suite 5, Boston, MA 02135 USA

Ancient Egypt Research Associates (AERA) is a 501(c) (3), tax-exempt, nonprofit organization dedicated to research on ancient Egypt at the Giza Plateau.

© 2009 by Ancient Egypt Research Associates, Inc.
Reprinted in 2011.

Layout by Alexandra Witsell.

Printed in Hollis, New Hampshire, by Puritan Press.

All rights reserved. No part of this publication may be reproduced, stored in a retrieval system or transmitted in any form or by any means, electronic, mechanical, photocopying, recording, or otherwise without the prior consent of the publisher.

ISBN: 0-9779370-8-9

Cover photo: The Khentkawes Monument with the pyramids of Khufu (right) and Khafre (left). The Khentkawes Town extends to right (east). Modern Cemetery lies in foreground. Photo by Mark Lehner. All photos in main excavation text are courtesy of Mark Lehner.

Contents

Acknowledgements

Deep gratitude goes to all of our benefactors for supporting our excavations, field school, and other programs. For major support for our 2008 field season we thank the Ann and Robert H. Lurie Foundation, David H. Koch Foundation, Charles Simonyi Fund for Arts and Sciences, Ted Waitt Family Foundation, Peter Norton Family Foundation, and the Myhrvold Family Charitable Foundation.

We are very grateful for the support of the Glen Dash Foundation, Marjorie Fisher, Ed and Kathy Fries, the Bill and Melinda Gates Foundation, J. Michael and Marybeth Johnston, Jason G. Jones and Emily E. Trenkner-Jones, Bruce and Carolyn Ludwig, David Marguiles, and Ann Thompson.

Our work would not have been possible without the additional support of Joseph F. Azrack, COSI Columbus, the Del Rio Family Foundation, Katie Ford, Michael and Janet Fourticq, Ed and Lorna Goodman, Glenn P. Hart, Frederick and Sydene Kober, Robert and Bonnie Larson, Buzz and Barbara McCoy, Ronald Nahas, Richard Redding, the Jon Q. and Ann S. Reynolds Fund, Seven Wonders Travel, Stephen Jay and Amy Sills, Jim and Sharon Todd, Julie Middleton, Barry J. West, Ray and Mary Arce, Henry Becton, Jr., James and Catherine Callard, James and Betsy Chaffin, Jr., Edgar M. and Elissa F. Cullman, James and Cynthia DeFrancia, Donna L. Dinardo, Phillip William Fisher, Hanley Family Charitable Fund, James and Mary Ann Harris, Rick and Kandy Holley, Brian Hunt, Significance Foundation-Brian and Alice Hyman Foundation, Clyde C. and Betsy Jackson, Jr., William C. and Victoria E. Johnston Family Foundation, Koss Family Fund, Dr. Susan and Mark R. Kroll Family Fund, Don Kunz, James and Dianne Light, George and Barbara von Liphart, Jr., Robert Lowe, Michael K. MacDonald, McLeod Family Trust, Edward Robert and Angette D. Meaney, Meyers Charitable Family Fund, Ambassador and Mrs. Charles T. Randt, Theresa L. Rudolph, Bonnie Sampsell, Robert M. Sharpe, George Sherman, Shiloh Foundation-Carol and Tom Wheeler, Craig and Nancy Smith, the Frank P. and Irene Stanek Fund, the Charles J. and Caroline Swindells Charitable Fund of the Oregon Community Foundation, Marilyn Taylor, C. Wendell and Mila Tewell, Robert M. Weekley, George and Pamela Willeford, John D. Wilson, and Susan Hudson Wilson, George Bunn, Jr., David Goodman, Charles and Wanda Guttas, Dan and Debby McGinn, Mary Perdue, the Rheinstein Family Trust, Harold G. Shipp, Kathryn Steinberg, Peter and Michele Serchuk, and Robin Young.

Our Egyptian and American Colleagues

For a very successful 2008 season, we are grateful to Dr. Zahi Hawass, Undersecretary of State and Secretary General of the Supreme Council of Antiquities (SCA). We thank Sabry Abd el-Aziz, General Director of Pharaonic Monuments; Atef Abu el-Dahab, Director of the Central Department of Pharaonic Monuments; Kamal Wahied, General Director of Giza Pyramids; and Mohammed Shiha, Chief Inspector of Giza Pyramids. We thank Mansour Boraik, General Director of Luxor; Sultan Eid, Director of Luxor Temple; Osama el-Shimy, Director of Saqqara; Samir Ghareeb, Supervisor of the Step Pyramid Project; and Affifi Roheim, Chief Inspector of Dahshur and Lisht and Supervisor of the Step Pyramid Project.

We are grateful to Magdi el-Ghandour, Director of the Foreign Missions Department, and Shaban Abd el-Gawad for their assistance. We also thank Mme. Amira Khattab and Amir Abd el-Hamid of the American Research Center in Egypt (ARCE) for their assistance. We would like to thank the following inspectors who represented the SCA at the sites: Gaber Abd El-Dayem, Nagla Zaki, and Ahmed Eiz at Giza; Eizzat Abu Bakr and Hanem Sadek in Luxor; Samir Ramadan and Mahrous el-Sanadeety at Saqqara.

We are grateful to Dr. Gil Stein, Director of the Oriental Institute, University of Chicago, and Dr. Larry Stager, Director of the Harvard Semitic Museum, for the support of their institutions. We also thank Dr. Joe Greene and Dr. James Armstrong of the Harvard Semitic Museum.

We thank Douglas Rawles and Mark Wakim of Reed Smith LLP for providing advice and counsel on a myriad of legal matters. Douglas, who has worked with AERA for over 12 years, continues to provide services on a pro bono basis, which is much appreciated by the AERA team.

Introduction

Ancient Egypt Research Associates (AERA)'s 2008 fieldwork included projects at three of Egypt's most famous archaeological sites: Giza, Saqqara, and Luxor.

We carried out the Salvage Archaeological Field School (SAFS) in Luxor with the American Research Center in Egypt (ARCE) and Egypt's Supreme Council of Antiquities (SCA) in order to both train SCA archaeologists in the real-world tension between urban development and archaeology, and to work with them to save as much archaeological information as possible in excavations on the Avenue of the Sphinxes in the site of the Khaled Ibn el-Waleed Garden as part of a broader project for urban and tourist development. The SAFS worked from January through March, with up to 150 archaeologists, students, workers, and support staff. During March, AERA directed major excavations and archaeological mapping projects in both Upper and Lower Egypt as the SAFS overlapped with our work at Giza.

At Giza, AERA worked in the Khentkawes Town (KKT) and at the site of the Menkaure (Third Pyramid) Valley Temple from March 1 until April 24, 2008. Because of a high water table, AERA did not excavate in our flagship Lost City site south of the Wall of the Crow (which we refer to in short as HeG, after *Heit el-Ghurab*, "Wall of the Crow" in Arabic). But we launched our Archaeological Science Program, where up to 30 specialists in ceramics, botany, zoology, lithics, and artifacts analyzed material culture from our excavations in the Lost City as a coordinated team focused on specific areas in line for final publication.

At Saqqara, AERA collaborated with the SCA and a Japanese consortium that included Osaka University, the Tokyo Institute of Technology, and the Ancient Orient Museum to survey and map the entire Djoser Step Pyramid using laser scanning and three-dimensional modeling between late May and early June. We helped produce this highly detailed and accurate record of Egypt's oldest pyramid ahead of major SCA restoration work that necessarily changed and masked large parts of the original fabric of this world heritage monument.

In May and June, AERA established at our Giza headquarters the Report Writing Tutorial for senior Egyptian supervisors of the SAFS. These graduates of the AERA/ARCE field schools worked with AERA field school instructors James Taylor and Freya Sadarangani to produce from the SAFS/Luxor excavation records a report for publication as a special supplement to the official SCA archaeological journal, *Annales du Service des Antiquités de l'Égypt* (*ASAE*).

In *Giza Occasional Papers 4* we summarize the 2008 work at Giza and Saqqara. We present new discoveries at the Khentkawes Town and the Menkaure Valley Temple, a preliminary scientific analysis of the osteological material from the Khentkawes Town, and a report on the Saqqara Laser Scanning Survey, which included a unique method of "capturing" all the complexities and detail of a gigantic monument and mapping the whole in three dimensions.

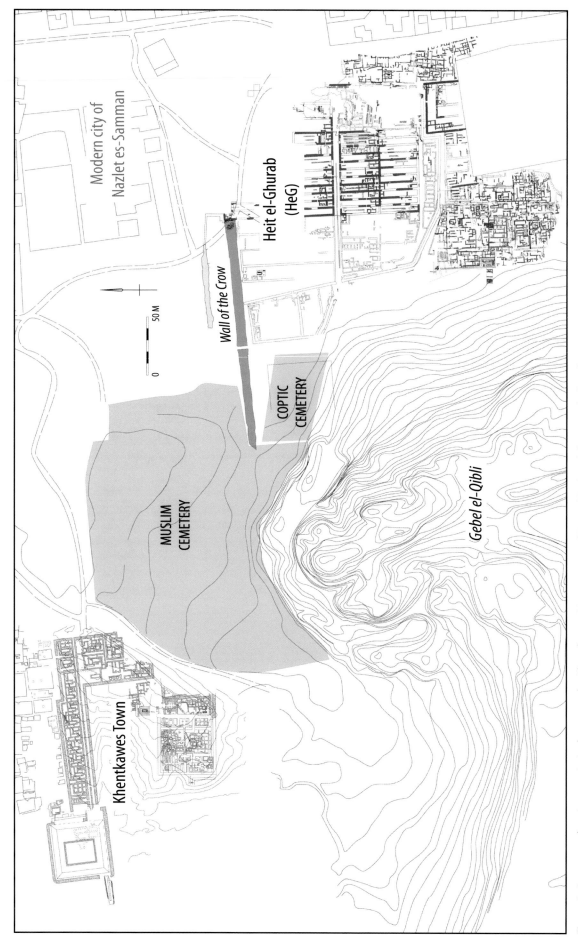

Figure 1. Area map showing proximity between the Khentkawes Monument and Town (KKT) and the Heit el-Ghurab site.

Figure 2. The Tomb of Queen Khentkawes in right center foreground of the Pyramids of Khufu (right), Khafre (center), and Menkaure (left). The Khentkawes Town (KKT) extends east (right) of the queen's monumental tomb. The modern cemetery fills the wadi at the southeast end of the quarry incline on which the builders founded the KKT. View to the northwest.

Excavations

The Khentkawes Town (KKT)

All the while we were excavating the Lost City of the Pyramids south of the Wall of the Crow (which we refer to in short as HeG, after *Heit el-Ghurab*, "Wall of Crow" in Arabic), we knew of a neighboring community, roughly contemporary with the final days of the ancient city, on the other side of the Wall of the Crow and a few hundred meters west: the town attached to the gigantic tomb of Khentkawes, an enigmatic queen who ruled at the end of the 4th Dynasty (figs. 1, 2). The form of her tomb is halfway between a *mastaba* (bench-like superstructure) and a pyramid, with a bedrock pedestal topped by a stack of laid blocks. Her titles, etched into the granite doorjambs of her chapel, only add to her mystery. They can be read either "Mother of the Two Kings of Upper and Lower Egypt," or "Mother of the King of Upper and Lower Egypt and King of Upper and Lower Egypt." The latter reading

suggests she ruled in the guise of a male pharaoh, as did Hatshepsut of the 18th Dynasty, one thousand years later.

We must assess our settlement south of the Wall of the Crow in the context of both the large urban agglomeration of KKT, and just 30 meters to the south of KKT, another settlement attached to the valley temple of the Pyramid of Menkaure (GIII.VT).

When Selim Hassan (1943) excavated the KKT in 1932 he found an L-shaped mudbrick settlement with modular houses strung out 150 m east-west along a causeway leading to the Khentkawes Monument (fig. 3). The foot of the L extends 61.5 m southward and contains larger buildings. The town covers an area 6,059 m square (measurements from Hassan's published map and text).

The modern, systemic methods that we use to excavate and record the HeG settlement did not exist in Selim Hassan's day, and so we know little about the KKT beyond its footprint as Hassan's surveyors mapped it. Hassan's

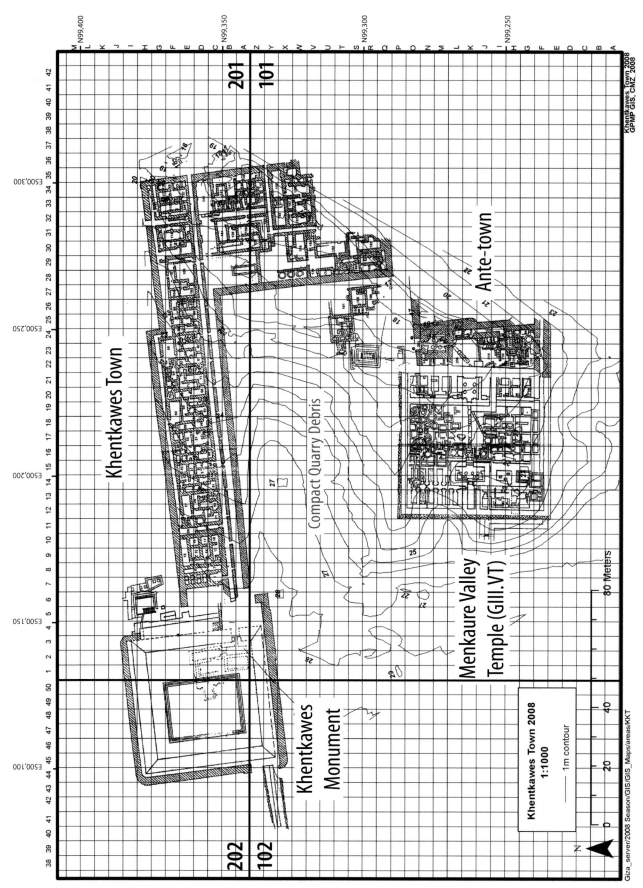

Figure 3. Contours of the KKT and GIII.VT prepared from the 2008 Survey. The contours reflect the fact that the ancient builders excavated areas for both the KKT and GIII.VT into a massive dump of limestone quarry debris, which still rises between the two zones to 27 m above sea level.

team did not retrieve and publish material culture, such as pottery, in a way that would inform us how long people occupied the KKT. Egyptologists assume the footprint dates to the late 4th Dynasty. Realizing the importance of the KKT for understanding the HeG site, we applied for the concession to resurvey KKT in 2004, but we only began to work there in 2005 when the site was under threat from construction of a new road and the high security wall around the modern cemeteries, which fill the wadi and stand between the HeG site and the KKT.

Discoveries of Earlier Seasons (Color Plate 1.1)

- *Season 2005*: Pieter Collet and Mark Lehner recorded the remnants of mudbrick walls in the western part of the foot of the town (KKT-F) around a large water tank (Water Tank 1) cut into the bedrock. They found that the builders created the foot of the town on two terraces. The higher western level was formed upon dumped limestone debris, waste from quarrying the bedrock. A long and narrow corridor, 1.50 m wide, led west along the southern sides of Houses K and L (see below, figs. 3, 4) to a flight of stairs leading up to the higher western terrace where the town builders made Water Tank 1, a series of round granaries, and magazines. Many of the mudbrick walls of these features were eroded down to the last few centimeters, sometimes millimeters, and sometimes completely scoured away in the 73 years since Hassan's crew found many of the walls waist-high or taller.

- *Season 2006*: We suspended clearing and mapping in the KKT, while our Giza Laser Scanning Survey team recorded the monument with laser scanners (Kawae 2007, 2009a).

- *Season 2007*: Lisa Yeomans and Pieter Collet worked in the eastern end of the KKT around the entrance to the causeway. In spite of the severe scouring of the walls, they found definite evidence of two building phases. The earlier phase included an entrance that was much wider than the 1.72-m wide causeway, with a limestone pivot socket 50 cm wide for a monumental swinging door (see page 35). Most surprising, they found the largely unexcavated remains of an eastern building, never mapped, beyond the 90° turn from the leg to the foot of the town. The lower-lying building appeared to be founded on a lower bedrock terrace. This building was not included on Selim Hassan's map, and does not show in any of the archival photographs from Hassan's work, or that of George Reisner who also worked at Giza during the 1930s.

Goals of Season 2008 (Color Plate 1.1)

Overlapping the month of March with the Advanced Field School (SAFS) in progress up in Luxor, we began the 2008 season at KKT with the following goals:

- *Buried building in KKT-E*: The previously undocumented buried building, east of the KKT, was a prime target of investigation in our Season 2008. In spite of a temptation to go straight after this discovery in a rather traditional way, we limited the season to six weeks because of the call to AERA to organize and direct the SAFS in Luxor, and because of a real need to catch up on analysis of material excavated over the years through the Archaeological Science Program that Dr. Mary Anne Murray directed in the Giza Field Laboratory.

- *Remains of KKT exposed by the previous excavations*: We also wanted to continue mapping whatever remained of the leg of the town (KKT-N), westward along the causeway to the queen's monumental tomb.

- *Interface between KKT and Menkaure Valley Temple*: As far as anyone knew from Hassan's 1932 excavation, the KKT was only occupied in the late 4th Dynasty. But people occupied the settlement within, and in front of, the Menkaure Valley Temple for the entire Old Kingdom, more than 300 years, as we knew from George Reisner's excavations from 1908 to 1910. Our 2005 clearing exposed a broad mud-paved ramp in the interface between the two settlements, which Hassan mentioned but no one had mapped. We hoped to trace the stratigraphic relationships between the south end of the KKT settlement and the Menkaure Valley Temple (GIII.VT), and to investigate the road leading east between them. We called this area KKT-AI.

- *Geophysical Survey of the Menkaure Valley Temple*: Except for a bit of the northeast corner, most of the Menkaure Valley Temple lies buried under Reisner's backfill, or sand that has drifted in over nearly a century. Glen Dash's 2007 geophysical survey signaled the continuation of the KKT east of its bend (Dash 2009) and the northern end of the lower mudbrick building, before Yeomans had this area cleared. We wanted a geophysical record of what might remain from the Valley Temple before we cleared it.

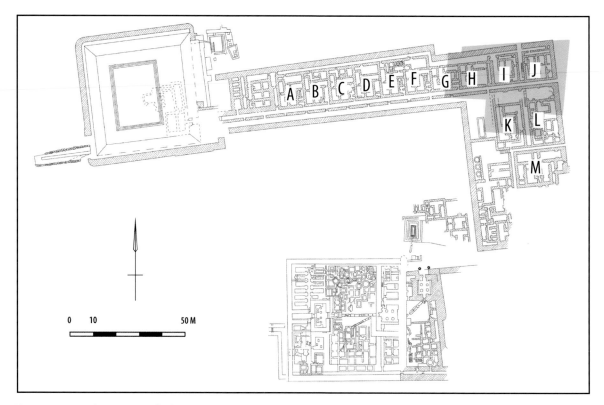

Figure 4. Letter designations for houses in KKT. Pieter Collet and Lisa Yeomans recorded the shaded area in 2007. In 2008 Collet worked in a 10 m-wide zone that took in the eastern half of House F and the western half of House G (Fig. 5a).

Team and Schedule

The KKT 2008 team included: Noha Bulbul (SCA), Pieter Collet, Delphine Driaux, Amelia Fairman, Mike House, Daniel Jones, Mark Lehner, Andrea Nevistic, Kasia Olchowska, Ana Tavares, Amanda Watts, Kelly Wilcox, and Hassan Mohammed Ramadan (SCA trainee). Gaber Abdel Dayem and Nagla Hafez served as inspectors for the Supreme Council of Antiquities (SCA). The remote sensing team included Glen and Joan Dash. Jessica Kaiser, Johnny Karlsson, Afaf Wahba (SCA), Ahmed Gabr (SCA), Amanda Agnew, Brianne Daniels, and Sandra Koch made up the osteoarchaeological team who excavated Late Period human burials.

We began our recording and partial excavation on Saturday March 1. We completed backfilling on Wednesday, April 24, 2008.

Recording and Mapping

- *Survey*: We prepared a contour map of the entire site that takes in the KKT and the Menkaure Valley Temple (GIII.VT) (fig. 3).

- *Geophysical Survey*: The remote sensing team prospected the entire area of the GIII.VT and the high mound of quarry debris between the GIII.VT and the leg of the KKT. They located the corners and other features of the GIII.VT excavated by Reisner in 1908–1910.

- *KKT and GIII.VT Mapping*: Our mapping is a complete archaeological recording, including maps at a large scale, 1:20, and sections and elevation drawings at 1:10. We expose and record what is left of the KKT in 10 × 10 m square areas. We document each exposure with photographs and assign stratigraphic feature numbers to every wall, deposit, and to cuts, such as pits and trenches. We complete an information form for each feature so designated. Whenever relevant, we excavate specific features either to clarify stratigraphic relationships or to collect archaeobotanical samples, pottery for dating, and any remaining material culture.

Excavations

We selected three main areas for excavation (Color Plate 1.1):

- *Area KKT-AI: The Interface:* We called this area, KKT-AI, "Amelia's Interface," after Amelia Fairman, who supervised work here. The boundaries of the Interface took in the road, or "Ramp," leading east immediately south of the KKT settlement and north of the GIII.VT; the northern end of the Ante-town that Selim Hassan found attached to the eastern front of the GIII.VT; the northeast corner of the GIII.VT; and the southern end of the KKT-F, the "foot" of the town. A massive, thick eastern wall (the "Glacis") bounds the Ante-town on the east (fig. 4, Color Plate 1.1). At the northern end of the Ante-town the Vestibule, with four alabaster column bases, opens to the Ramp.

- *Dan's Cut:* Daniel Jones excavated along the north-south line in KKT-F between the upper terrace of dumped quarry debris on the west and the lower mudbrick walls on the east. Initially it appeared that the builders made the lower KKT structures (houses?) first, with marl plaster and some buttresses on the western face of a common mudbrick wall, and created the upper terrace later by dumping quarry debris up against that face. Someone—we thought Selim Hassan's excavators—dug trenches along the line of the plastered face, hence our term "Dan's Cut." The cut skipped over those walls of the later phase that ran across from the lower to the upper terrace.

- *Area KKT-E:* Mark Lehner and Kasia Olchowska excavated immediately east of the eastern end of the Khentkawes Causeway to investigate the buried building east of KKT.

Results and Discoveries of KKT 2008

Even with only a six-week field season, we harvested much information. We describe our results from north to south, and then return to the north to review our findings east of the Khentkawes Town, our Area KKT-E.

Mapping Houses in KKT-North (KKT-N)

The town of Queen Khentkawes consists of one row of large "priest" houses along the northern side of the causeway, which leads from her funerary monument to a large building (her valley temple?) on the east (see below, KKT-E). This northern strip has six large houses on the west (Houses A–F), and four smaller houses on the east (Houses G–J, fig. 4).

In 2007 Yeomans and Collet recorded the scanty remains of the eastern houses. The two houses furthest northeast (I–J) have long, east-west storage magazines at the back (north) partly built into North Street and narrowing the passage. This street runs along the ten houses north of the causeway.

During our 2008 season Collet continued mapping KKT-N westward in a north to south strip, 10 m wide and 30 m long adjacent to the area recorded in 2007 (figs. 5a, 5b). This swath included the northern enclosure wall, North Street, part of House F, the causeway, South Street, and the southern enclosure wall. On the north of Collet's 2008 patch, the northern enclosure wall and North Street

jog north and then continue west, making the town wider from this point on (the houses to the west of this point are longer than those to the east).

The boundaries of Collet's cleaning and mapping were those of our grid squares, rather than the boundaries of the houses, so his work took in the eastern part of House F and the western part of House G, rooms 86 to 95 on Hassan's 1932 map (fig. 5a). The part of House F that Collet recorded showed at least two phases of use and rebuilding. Houses F and G show characteristic features of Giza houses, such as zigzag entrances, secluded rooms with niches that might have been for sleeping rooms (Room 85 in House F and 95 in House G), and long and narrow storage magazines (Room 90). House F had a wide courtyard at the north. The walls were much eroded, but the footprint remained.

Noha's House (K)

Giza Inspector and 2007 Field School student, Noha Bulbul, continued recording House K on the lower terrace of the leg of KKT. Yeomans and Collet mapped the northern part of House K in 2007. We took to calling it "Noha's House" (figs. 6, 7a, 8).

It is noteworthy that the western wall of Noha's House (K) showed evidence for an early phase of KKT, pre-dating the causeway. The plaster line of this wall continues northward across, and under, the remains of the causeway walls (Yeomans 2007). The plaster line of the western wall of House K aligns with the western wall of House I. This suggests that Houses I and K belonged to a common complex, along with Houses J and L on the east, that predated the causeway. The western wall of Noha's House is also one segment of the common wall alignment along "Dan's Cut" (see below).

In spite of belonging to a larger complex, "Noha's House" is isolated as a discrete unit by a large open court on the north, between the House K and the causeway; by a corridor, 1.40 m wide on the south, running due west from the lower town to a stairway up to the higher terrace with open courts and granaries along the western side of the KKT foot; and by a street, 2.10 m wide, along the east (figs. 6, 7a). The evidence from our 2007 work indicates that this street existed as part of the earlier phase, prior to the causeway, and that after the east-west causeway was laid across the north-south street, masons cut the tunnel in order to cross underneath.

Set off by these features, Noha's House measures 13.40 m north-south × 10.20 m, 137 m square, or 213 m square if we include the open court to the north. This by itself is a good-sized house compared to houses we found in the HeG settlement south of the Wall of the Crow, but only half of or less than the 400-m-square of House Unit 1 in the Western Town (Kawae 2009b).

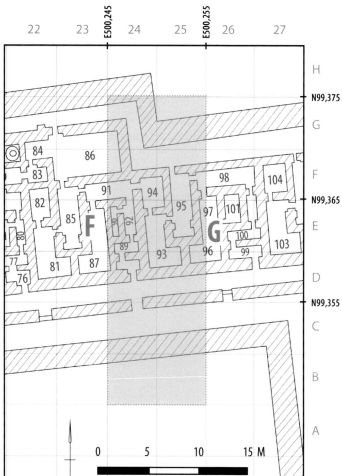

Figure 5a (left). Houses F and G with room numbers from Hassan's map. In 2008 Pieter Collet recorded Rooms 86 on the west to 96 on the east (gray overlay).

Figure 5b (below). Pieter Collet's 10 × 30-m swath of clearing and recording in KKT-N. View to the south.

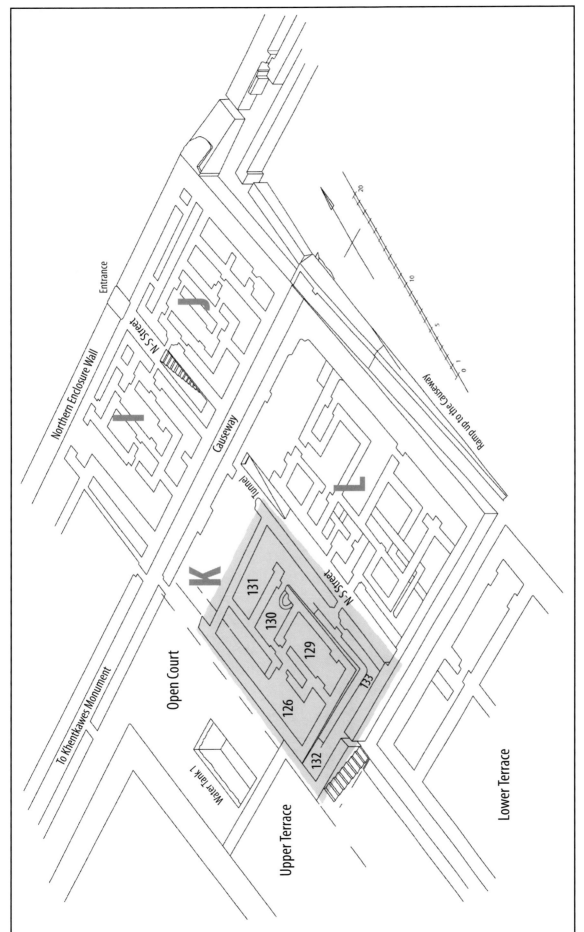

Figure 6. Isometric of KKT in 2008. Noha's House (House K) indicated in gray shading. Original isometric drawing by Mark Lehner.

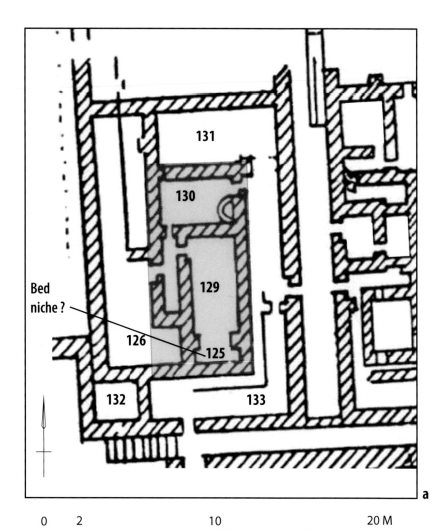

131

130

129

Bed
niche ?

126

125

132   133

a

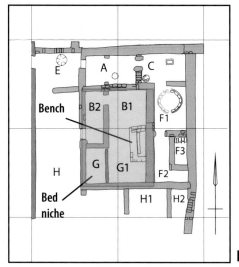

b

Bench

E

A   C

B2   B1

F1

H

G   G1

F3
F2

Bed
niche

H1   H2

Figure 7a. Noha's House (House K) with room numbers from Hassan's map.

Figure 7b. Plan of the Eastern Town House in the HeG settlement.

Figure 7c. Plan of House Unit 1 in Area SFW.

Note similarity in the plans, all at the same scale, where broader rooms/open courts surround a core house (areas shaded in gray: Rooms 129, 130, and small unnumbered vestibule on west in Noha's House; Rooms B1-B2, Room G-G1 in ETH plan; Room 10,780 with sleeping platform in SFW.H1).

0   2   10   20 M

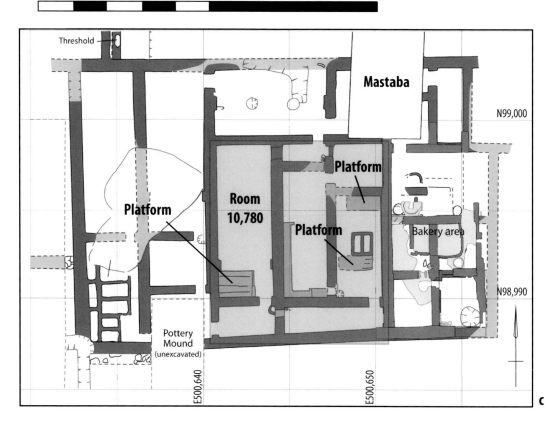

Threshold

Mastaba

N99,000

Platform

Platform

Room
10,780

Platform

Bakery area

N98,990

Pottery
Mound
(unexcavated)

E500,640

E500,650

c

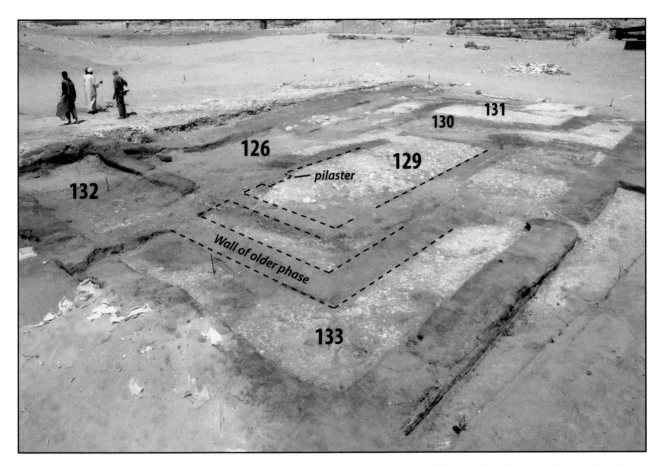

Figure 8. Noha's House cleared, view to the northwest. Corridor 133 is in the foreground. Room 129 in the center shows a floor level raised with limestone debris. The southeast corner of the core house shows an underlying, older phase projecting into Corridor 133 (foreground).

Like House Unit 1 (fig. 7c), House κ included a large rectangular room (Hassan's Room 129) oriented north-south with pilasters at the southern end defining a niche (Room 125), which we might suspect was for a bed platform such as Yukinori Kawae found in Room 10,780 in House Unit 1. Compare Room 129, measuring 7.40 north-south × 2.60 east-west, with the large room 10,780 in House Unit 1 measuring 8.5 m north-south × 3.0 m east-west (figures 7a, 7c). The bed platform in House Unit 1 filled the 1.32-m width of the niche defined by the pilasters. The niche (Room 125) was only 1 m wide. Noha found a good footprint of the western pilaster, while the eastern one had been scoured away.

The hypothetical bedroom (129), a small room to the north (130), and a narrow vestibule on the west, form a kind of core of House κ (fig. 7a) with a floor level raised by limestone debris about 40 cm over the level of a corridor (133) along the south and east, and over the floor of Room 126 on the west. Room 130 still shows traces of an oven against the eastern wall, as indicated on Hassan's map (fig. 7a). To enter the core house and sleeping room (129) one passed through a doorway, about 70 cm wide like most of the doorways in House κ, through the eastern wall

(which is the same as the western wall of the north-south avenue, see fig. 6), turned right into the corridor (133), then left into the room (130), with the oven, then left into the long narrow (1 m wide) vestibule, then left again into Room 129. The various doorways and turns are similar to the entrance of the bedroom in House Unit 1 (fig. 7c).

It is possible that Hassan's excavators removed limestone debris that also raised the floor level of the corridor (133), because some such debris still exists in the northern end. When Hassan's excavators cleared the southern end and westward turn of the corridor (133), they exposed mudbrick walls forming the southeast corner of an earlier phase of the structure. The underlying walls are set off into the corridor one wall-width from the walls of the southeast corner of the later phase. Hassan's cartographer mapped the earlier phase walls as an unfilled line in contrast to the hachured fill of the mudbrick walls of the main phase. According to Hassan's map, the earlier eastern wall of House κ includes a jamb making an entrance into the southern end of corridor 133 just inside and to the left (south) of the main eastern doorway onto the north-south avenue. The traces of the earlier walls suggest that the core of

House ĸ had been nearly leveled and rebuilt during the life of the settlement.

Corridor 133 flanks the core house on the east and south in a reversed ʟ-pattern. A broader corridor-like room flanks the entire western side of the core rooms. Hassan's map is ambiguous here, and seems to show remnants of a large rectangular room on the northwest of this space—the lines may again show two superimposed phases. The western corridor ends at an ʟ-shaped turn on the south into Room 126. The corridor on the west, Room 131 on the north, and Corridor 133 on the east and south surround a core unit of about 67 m square that contains the vestibule, oven room, and hypothetical bedroom. In this respect House ĸ is similar to the Eastern Town House in the HeG settlement, where broader rooms or open courts surround a core house (fig. 7b). More investigation is needed in the western side of House ĸ, which was beyond Noha's 2008 work, to clarify the overall layout.

"Dan's Cut:" The Terraced Town (KKT-F)

The boundary between the upper terrace and lower town is not indicated on Hassan's map, but shows very distinctly on site (figs. 9, 10). We discovered in 2005 that the builders founded the western part of the "foot," or southern town (ĸĸᴛ-ꜰ), on a higher terrace of dumped limestone debris. Initially, we thought that the builders made the terrace after building an alignment of walls that includes the western wall of House ĸ. On the surface the western face of this wall shows a marl render with a lighter, near-white, thinner coat of plaster, and it appears that the limestone debris forming the upper terrace banked against that rendered face (fig. 10). This itself would suggest major building phases in the ĸĸᴛ, as opposed to it being a synchronic, discrete urban footprint.

At some point—we thought during Selim Hassan's 1932–1933 excavations—someone dug a series of trenches through the limestone debris along the western face of

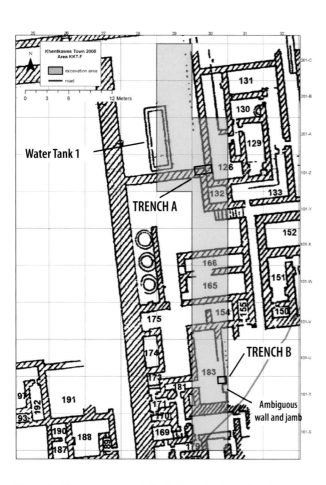

Figure 9. The zone of "Dan's Cut" along the boundary between the lower (right) and upper (left) terraces in the KKT foot (KKT-F) overlaid on a modified version of Hassan's map, which does not show the terrace boundary or wall that runs along it.

Figure 10. View to the south along the boundary between lower (left) and upper (right) terraces, marked on north by marl render with white plaster line. Quarry debris of upper terrace banks against the plastered wall face.

Figure 11. Dan Jones in Trench A along the boundary between the lower terrace (left) and upper terrace (right). The series of older trenches along the upper terrace can be seen in the background. View to the south.

the mudbrick walls along this line (fig. 11). The trenches stop at walls that cross from the lower town—where the walls are preserved higher—to the upper terrace, such as the wall south of Water Tank 1 (fig. 9), or the walls of the magazines (Rooms 165, 166) east of the round granaries in Hassan's plan. The trenches then pick up again on the other side of these cross walls. It appeared to us that the trench excavators sought to explore and expose the plastered faces of the thick north-south mudbrick walls along this line (fig. 10), but became confused by the cross walls founded on a deeper level in the lower town, and extending across to the upper terrace.

On the other hand, at places it looked like the cross walls spanned trenches that were dug before the cross walls had been built (in a later phase?), and at those points the builders bridged the trenches with large, irregular

limestone fill, just where the walls crossed to the upper terrace.

Hassan's map glosses over all these distinctive features (fig. 9). The mudbrick wall along this line in the north, which is the western wall of House κ, is thicker (1.70 m) than in Hassan's map. Alongside it on the west his cartographer put a dotted line, about where the edge of the upper terrace is located. He or she picks up this dotted line along the same alignment toward the southern end of the κκτ foot, and now, to the west of the dotted line, leaves a line indicating the eastern face of a wall that then becomes the western face of a wall, with a projecting jamb, along the east of Room 183 (fig. 9). The mapmaker did not know how to incorporate the complexities of the terraces, the different phases, and the cuts of the trenches in a synchronic schematic of the κκτ footprint.

Figure 12. Dan Jones points to a wide foundation of a mudbrick wall built upon bedrock with two outer faces and a rubble-filled core in the northern Trench A. A thinner, later wall flanked by fill rests upon the older foundation. View to south.

To sort this out, Daniel Jones took on the task of recording relationships between the upper and lower terraces, and the cut along this interface. Jones excavated two small trenches, A and B, down the line of this interface (figs. 9, 11, 12). In both trenches he discovered that builders founded segments of mudbrick walls along this common alignment on a prepared bedrock surface that extends westward under the limestone debris comprising the upper terrace. The surface in Trench B, to the south, is 30 to 40 cm lower than in Trench A due to the natural south-southeast dip of the natural limestone strata. When the quarrymen removed blocks from the harder limestone layers prior to the building of the town, they followed the yellowish clay-rich beds, because these layers are softer and it is easier to cut out blocks from the intervening harder layers. By this practice they followed the natural geological dip to the south-southeast.

In both Trenches A and B, Jones found that the builders cut into the limestone fill of the upper, western terrace to found the mudbrick walls, so that fill layer must have existed somewhat farther east before they erected the mudbrick walls flush against the vertical cut through the debris. It might be the case that the builders did not so much create the upper western terrace for the foot of

the KKT by dumping limestone quarry debris for that purpose, as they leveled the lower eastern edge of the huge mound of such debris that fills the entire rectangular area between the east-west leg of the KKT and the GIII.VT. That is, they cut into the debris to level it and to make the step down from the higher to the lower terraces. Our work this season shows that people also cut the debris back for building the extramural houses west of the southern end of the KKT foot, probably in a later phase.

In the northern Trench A, the first phase wall [21,888] consists of two thick mudbrick faces with a rubble core, wider at bottom (fig. 12). The wall [29,957] in the southern Trench B is entirely brick-built. Within Trenches A and B Jones found no additions to the wall, such as the render seen farther north (fig. 10), which suggested the limestone debris there did bank against an earlier standing wall after masons plastered its western face.

Jones found evidence that the occupants of the settlement repaired these walls. In both trenches he discovered a cut [29,324] where they removed limestone debris of the upper terrace fill for a width of 60 cm, sloping their cut down to the east to expose the western face of wall [21,888]. They filled gaps in the wall, "tuck-pointing" with rubble (pottery, stone, charcoal), then re-smoothed the face, and refilled the trench they made along the face of the wall.

Later, the occupants leveled the southern wall [29,957] to build a new, thinner (84 cm thick) wall [21,909] directly upon the older one. They added at least two buttresses protruding 40 cm from the western face of the new, thinner wall [21,909]. The repairs and the various rebuilds of most of these walls, as well as many of the structures still visible, suggest that the town was long-lived.

At the end of the season Jones concluded that the series of narrow trenches along the interface between the upper terrace and lower town, was ancient (fig. 11), made primarily for the rebuilds and repairs on the mudbrick walls along this line. Selim Hassan's workers had emptied the ancient trenches of material back-filled by those who repaired the walls in the time that people lived in the settlement.

While Jones worked, Andrea Nevistic and Delphine Driaux, later joined by Pieter Collet, completed the recording of most of the entire southern area of the L-shaped town, including the upper terrace and lower structures on the east. Amanda Watts and Kelly Wilcox

completed the recording of the houses, such as the Fieldstone House (see below), outside and west of the western enclosure wall. These extramural structures are mostly built with undressed limestone blocks and seem to be of a later phase.

The KKT-GIII.VT Interface

As stated above, one of the main aims this season was to record stratigraphic links between the Khentkawes Town (KKT) and the Menkaure Valley Temple (GIII.VT).

In 1908, a hundred years almost to the month before our work in 2008, Reisner excavated the Valley Temple of Menkaure and recovered magnificent artifacts and statuary. Little was known then of the various elements that comprised a pyramid complex (typically an upper temple, causeway, valley temple, boat pits, and subsidiary pyramids). Reisner found the GIII.VT by extrapolating the axis of the causeway from the Upper Temple down to the east. He excavated the different phases of the temple and the settlement within its walls (Reisner 1931). He established that Menkaure had conceived his valley temple on a massive scale comparable to the valley temple

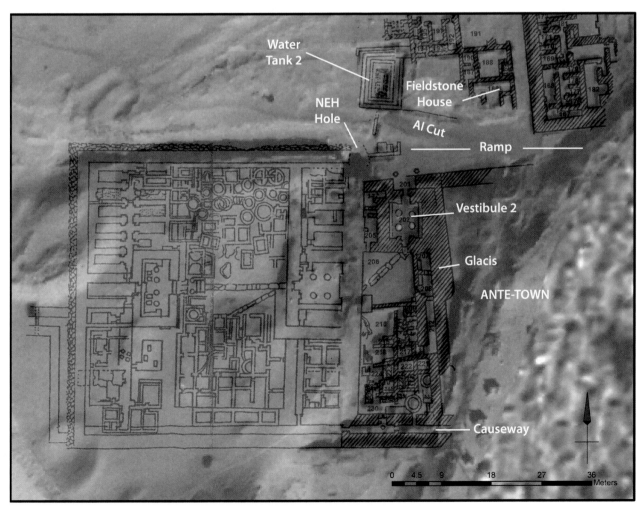

Figure 13. Area KKT-AI and GIII.VT from a georeferenced Royal Air Force aerial photo and overlaid Hassan and Reisner maps.

built of monolithic blocks by Khafre to the northeast. The masonry work, involving large limestone blocks weighing several tons, stopped with Menkaure's premature death. Workers under his successor, Shepseskaf, finished the upper temple, causeway, and valley temple in plastered mudbrick. Reisner investigated two major phases of the GIII.VT building and the complex domestic structures that invaded the façade and courtyard of the GIII.VT. In 1932, more than a decade after Reisner's last work in the GIII.VT, Selim Hassan (1943) extended his excavations of the KKT southwards to the front, eastern part of the valley temple.

The GIII.VT Ante-town

At the eastern front of the GIII.VT Selim Hassan's 1932 crew excavated more of the small mudbrick chambers and bins where Reisner had cleared and mapped only a few against the southeast corner of the GIII.VT. Hassan found a complex of such structures, along with an open court in front of the center of the GIII.VT, and a limestone-paved path leading to a second vestibule with four alabaster column bases similar to the vestibule just inside the original GIII.VT entrance, except this one opened north. The parallel walls of the original Menkaure causeway corridor, exiting east from its run along the southern side of the GIII.VT, contained this ensemble on the south (fig. 13). The unusually thick and accreted walls of the second vestibule closed off the ensemble on the north, and a mudbrick wall, thickened in two or more phases, contained this agglomeration on the east. In Hassan's map one of the accretions of the latter wall has a rounded end, giving the appearance of a fortification. When we cleared the face of this eastern wall in 2005, it was so stout and sloped so dramatically from elevation 19.25 to 16.00, that we called it "the Glacis." The Glacis certainly raises the question as to how one approached and ascended to the GIII.VT original entrance before this addition.

Hassan considered this ensemble, 18.5 m wide east-west at its southern end, to be the valley temple of the Khentkawes funerary complex, even though it has no connection to her causeway. Kemp (1983; 1989; 2006) was surely correct in seeing this cluster as an extension of the GIII.VT town, separate from the KKT. We took to calling it the Ante-town (as in "in front of," rather than "before" in a temporal sense).

In 2008 Amelia Fairman supervised work in the area from the southern end of the KKT foot to the vestibule in the Ante-town (see below), taking in the broad roadway or ramp that ascends toward the northeast corner of the GIII.VT between the two towns (fig. 14). We called this area KKT-AI, for "Amelia's Interface." Later in the season Mike House came up from the SAFS in Luxor to assist. Kelly Wilcox and Amanda Watts also worked in KKT-AI.

The Ramp

Hassan's map shows both the KKT and the GIII.VT with its Ante-town (figs. 3, 4), but leaves them unconnected by a blank strip. Hassan described the so-called Khentkawes valley temple "at the southeastern corner of a open area bounded on the north and east by the girdle wall of the city" (1943: 53). By this he meant the huge rectangular area between the GIII.VT and the leg of the KKT. This area is not a courtyard. Rather a huge mound of compact limestone quarry waste fills it (fig. 3). Nevertheless Hassan continued: "Access to this courtyard is gained by means of a broad causeway running westwards from the valley and lying between a thick mudbrick wall attached to the (Khentkawes) Valley-Temple and the (southern) girdle wall of the City (KKT)" (Hassan 1943: 53).

In 2005 we exposed for a length of 9 m this "causeway," which is a substantial and monumental ramp composed of silt paving layers over a core or foundation of limestone debris between mudbrick walls (Lehner, Kamel, and Tavares 2006: 16). Our clearing this season exposed 21 m of the ramp, from its lowest exposure on the east where it disappears under the road and cement security wall made in 2004 around the modern cemetery to a huge hole (NEH) [29,810] that someone excavated through the ramp near the northeast corner of the GIII.VT (see below). Our clearing showed that the silt-paved surface of the roadway continues westward, passing the northern side of the NEH excavation and continuing along the northern side of the GIII.VT for at least another 7 m to the west. The Ramp rises 1.13 m on a run of 20 m, a slope of about 6°.

An east-west mudbrick wall, 1.55 m thick, forms the southern shoulder of the ramp. This wall drops steeply from 17.75 to 16.00 m, like the Glacis of the Ante-town to which it attaches perpendicularly. The northern edge of the ramp is a long, irregular trench, the AI Cut (AIC) that may have resulted from someone robbing out a northern bounding mudbrick wall matching the one along the southern side of the ramp (see below). Traces of this wall gave a width of 1.40 m. Where it is missing, the alluvial mud pavement of the ramp ends abruptly along the irregular edge of the AIC.

Whereas the southern wall of the ramp runs roughly east-west, the trench or cut along the northern side of the ramp angles to the northwest up the slope of the site. This gives the impression that the ramp broadened out as it rose to the west. The ramp is 6.70 m wide between its southern wall and the cut at the lowest and easternmost point we could measure near the limit of the clearing, broadening to 10.40 m wide about midway into our cleared area.

Runnels in the Ramp

The surface of the ramp is concave in cross-section, with the longer, more gradual slope on the north down to the

Figure 14. Area KKT-AI. Early in the season before we removed the post-1932 sand from the Vestibule, from the NEH hole at the northeast corner of the Menkaure Valley Temple, and from a 10 × 10 m square on the south side of Water Tank 2 about where the geophysical team carries out a radar survey. View to the west.

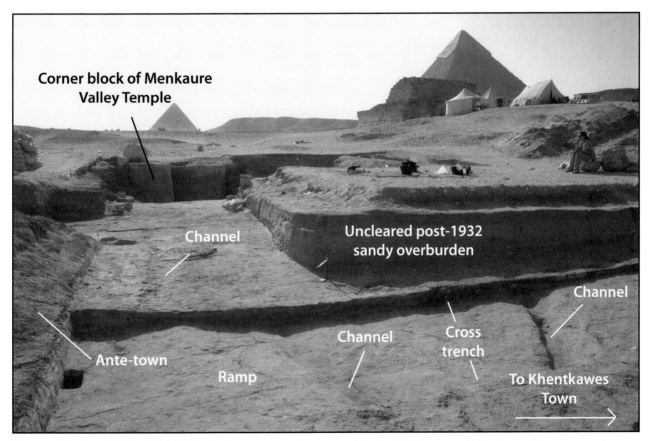

Figure 15. The Ramp in Area KKT-AI with shallow cross trench excavated by Amelia Fairman and Mike House. The uppermost alluvial silt-paved concave surface shows a faint channel parallel to the southern wall. Two other channels show in the lower surface exposed in the trench. View to the west.

lowest point of the concavity more to the south side. The intent appears to have been that rainwater would flow both east and toward the south side and this is evidenced by runnels and drains that run closer to the south side. One possible channel shows in the alluvial mud paving that Hassan exposed, running roughly parallel to the southern wall of the Ramp and about 75 cm north of that wall (fig. 15).

House and Fairman exposed two other channels in a shallow trench, 2 m wide, that they excavated across the width of the Ramp to look for successive paving layers, and to get the stratigraphic connections north and south. Running water might have cut the northernmost of these two channels, which trends northwest-southeast. The southern channel in this surface, 20 cm lower than the Ramp surface that Hassan exposed, is better prepared. It is oriented slightly more northeast-southwest. At 30 cm wide, it is reminiscent of the Main Street channel in the settlement south of the Wall of the Crow (Abd el-Aziz 2007: 123–125), flanked by a thin alluvial mud render and similarly composed over crushed marl limestone.

These channels could be clues to the meaning of the great cut or trench along the southern side of the ramp (see below).

Massive Foundation

We saw the foundation for the upper, western end of the Ramp in a deep excavation (NEH, fig. 16), which someone made long before our time at the northeast corner of the GIII.VT. Ana Tavares supervised the clearing and recording of this prior excavation (given the AERA feature number [29,810]) during our 2008 season.

The roadbed of the Ramp continues past the entrance of the second vestibule and to the edge of the previous excavation [29,810], which cut through the Ramp and exposed layers of limestone rubble of 2.46 m combined thickness that are either an accretion holding back other material, or, more likely, the very foundation layers that people dumped to build up the Ramp (fig. 16). We investigated this point further by dissecting these layers. The large limestone rubble of the lower layer is similar to layers filling 4th Dynasty construction ramps elsewhere at

Figure 16. View to east showing the west-facing section of the NEH hole [29,810] at the northeast corner of the GIII.VT through the massive limestone rubble foundation of the Ramp. The mudbrick casing and limestone core blocks of the northeast corner of the GIII.VT show at lower right. The ramp passes the Vestibule entrance (upper center) and along the northern side of the GIII.VT.

Figure 17. The portico of the second Vestibule at the upper, western end of the Ramp, flanked by limestone bases for two thin columns, opens into the northern end of the GIII.VT Ante-town. Only the eastern part (left) of the Vestibule interior was emptied of post-1932 fill. View to the south.

Figure 18. Entrance threshold of the second Vestibule, with limestone uprights that formed the jambs. The circular and square sockets might have received a vertical entrance bolt.

Giza, which prompts us to ask: was this Ramp first built for construction purposes, to deliver material, possibly granite blocks for cladding Menkaure's Upper Temple, from the east?

The Vestibule

The Ramp or roadway makes sense of the second Vestibule and the fact that it is turned almost 90° to the north from the east-west center axis of the GIII.VT. With the development of the Ante-town and Glacis, no direct approach led straight on into the first Vestibule in the front center of the GIII.VT. Instead, one ascended the broad Ramp, turned left (south), and then passed through a portico, 3.85 m wide, between two thin columns, 26 cm and 28 cm in diameter on the east and west respectively as measured from the sockets in limestone pads still in place (fig. 17).

The columns rose at the outer corners of a recess forming a small portico with a limestone threshold still *in situ*. A pivot and socket in the limestone threshold suggested a swinging double leaf door (fig. 18). The limestone slabs that formed the jambs of the entrance doorway remain *in situ* and close to their original positions.

Fairman and House excavated deposits, left by Selim Hassan, filling the vestibule of the Ante-town (figs. 19a, 19b). The team removed the post-1932 fill from the eastern two-thirds of the Vestibule, exposing the two eastern alabaster column bases, with diameters of about a meter (2 cubits) and the eastern edge of the western column bases (fig. 19a). Center to center, the columns bases are spaced 2.10 m (4 cubits).

Fairman and House excavated a half-section through the vestibule floor exposing earlier domestic installations

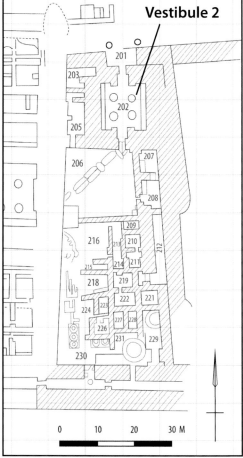

Figure 19a. The second vestibule floor quartered with floors excavated in diagonal quarters. Fairman and House excavated through a thick rebuild or accretion of the interior eastern wall. View to the north.

Figure 19b. Plan of Ante-town, after Hassan 1943. Photo shows the room marked "202" on the plan.

Figure 20. Mike House and Kelly Wilcox excavate round sockets for ceramic vessels sunk through overlaying silty floors and down into a crushed marl bedding. People who inhabited the Vestibule installed the jars around the alabaster column bases. View to the southeast.

(fig. 20). Their work revealed a complex and long-lived occupation, with an intricate sequence of floors and wall remodeling. They excavated to the foundation of one column base and found it has a roughly finished "skirt" embedded in marl and limestone chips over which occupants laid several floors of alluvial silt during the course of their occupation. The floor was well kept and resurfaced various times. A series of storage jars were set into the floor when people occupied the temple vestibule. People made a number of pot emplacements in these floors, cutting down into the foundation layer (fig. 20). One contained a nearly intact vessel. Both Reisner and Hassan had excavated houses within the Menkaure Valley Temple. The village that developed within this temple spans 300 years, from the time when our main site south of the Wall of the Crow was occupied to the end of the Old Kingdom.

Fairman and House extended the half-section north from the temple vestibule to the Ramp (fig. 17). Then they linked it to a long north-south section through the road surfaces of the Ramp (fig. 15). This showed that the Ramp was repaired and resurfaced. They found that the uppermost layers from resurfacing the Ramp are later than the render run, or seal, up against the bottom of the

plastered northern face of the Vestibule northern wall, which means those surfaces were laid down later, but the Ramp and Vestibule must have functioned together in at least the later phases of occupation.

Fairman and House found plastered floors that lipped up to both earlier and later internal faces of the eastern wall of the Vestibule. They cut back a section in the inner face of the eastern Vestibule wall and found that it has been thickened with rebuilds and additions (fig. 19a). A major additional wall with a rubble-filled core thickened the wall and reduced the interior space. Altogether, successive remodeling thickened this wall's interior by 1.69 m. Along with the thickening of the external wall forming a kind of glacis, the Vestibule came to be embedded in a mass of mudbrick. The excavators noted: "…one likely explanation for (the internal accretion) may be that following the removal or reuse of the columns, a smaller internal space needed to be created in order to support a roof" (Fairman 2008: 2).

Water Tank 2
Water Tank 2 is a north-south rectangular basin cut into the bedrock, surrounded by fieldstone walls retaining a rubble core. This created a series of steps, or narrow

Figure 21. Delphine Driaux (upper left) maps the limestone retaining walls of Water Tank 2 sunk into quarry debris at the higher level (upper right). Ana Tavares (right) stands on the silt-paved surface of the Ramp and maps the edge of the hole (NEH) at the northeast corner of the GIII.VT. The workers are removing post-1932 fill from the NEH. View to the northwest.

Figure 22. Delphine Driaux maps the southern shoulder of Water Tank 2, which rises 1.40 m higher than the level of the top of the Ramp on which Driaux stands. The Vestibule lies in the background. View to the southeast.

terraces, leading down into the tank. Our clearing of the post-1932 overburden in a 10 × 10-m grid square north of the GIII.VT northeast corner exposed the southern terrace/wall of this feature, as well as the mouth of a drain leading from the tank onto the Ramp. Selim Hassan related this drain to a plastered mudbrick building that he designated as the embalming tent for Khentkawes' funerary rites. We exposed part of a wall of this building this season. We would like to excavate further north and east to investigate these structures.

We refer to this basin as Water Tank 2 to distinguish it from the other rectangular basin, Water Tank 1, cut into the bedrock and through the quarry debris forming the upper terrace in the western side of the KKT foot (fig. 6). This season we only cleared the southern shoulder of the massive limestone retaining walls that surround Water Tank 2 (figs. 21, 22).

While those who made Water Tank 2 cut it down into the limestone bedrock, they also built two massive limestone revetment walls to shore up the quarry debris on its southern side to a height 1.40 m higher than the silt-paved roadbed of the Ramp. The result is a three-step interior for the basin. If it filled to about the level of the roadbed, water could be let out through a drain, which we partially exposed, leading southwards across the roadbed toward an installation with a bench in front of the northeast corner of the GIII.VT. If the basin is indeed a water tank, the retaining walls raise its brim above the general floor levels of the extramural Fieldstone House, and the KKT-F floors. These floors are themselves about 80 cm higher than the floor of the Vestibule and the top of the Ramp.

Next season we plan to expose more of Water Tank 2 and remove the post-1932 fill from a 10-m grid square between our exposure of the southern shoulder of the basin and the Fieldstone House to the east of it.

The Enigmatic AI Cut (AIC)

A long, ragged trench trending east-southeast to north-northwest along the northern side of the Ramp is a major feature of Area KKT-AI, and it frustrates our efforts to determine the stratigraphic relationships in the interface

Figure 23. The AI Cut (AIC) is an irregular trench, broadening to the east, between the Ramp on the south (left), and the Fieldstone House on the north (right). A short segment of the northern wall of the Ramp remains (center, top) extending from the section through the sand at top center of the photograph. The AIC extends west, upslope, as far as the southern shoulder of Water Tank 2, just in front of the striding team members (upper left). View to the west.

Figure 24. The AI Cut (AIC) in the interface, view to the north. Workers excavate sandy limestone gravel that fills the northern side of the Cut. The enclosure wall of the KKT foot is on the east (far right). The floor levels of the extramural Fieldstone House (center) are 80 cm higher than the level of the Ramp on the south (lower left) where it passes the house. At center far left: a remnant of the northern wall of the ramp, molded in quarry debris.

between the KKT and the GIII.VT (figs. 23, 24). It is as though some force severed the stratigraphic relations between the KKT and GIII.VT exactly where we had hoped to find the link!

At first we thought that Hassan's workers might have cut this irregular trench, which we dubbed the AI Cut (AIC), but his map shows the abrupt termination of walls along this line, suggesting the cut preceded his excavation, and is therefore ancient. For example the AIC appears to have cut through the entirety of the extramural Fieldstone House immediately west of the southwest corner of the KKT foot (figs. 14, 23, 24). Whatever force made the AIC also cut down through the limestone quarry debris forming the upper western terrace in which both the foot of KKT and the Fieldstone House are founded (fig. 24). We considered the possibility that the AIC was the trench whereby someone took out most of the northern wall of the Ramp.

We traced the AIC for a distance of 16.20 m along the northern side of the Ramp, from our limit of excavation on the lower eastern end where it runs under the modern road and cemetery, to the upper western end, where we cleared

the southern end of Water Tank 2. The Cut is narrow (1.20 to 1.60 m wide) where it runs across the southern shoulder of the massive, infilled Water Tank 2 retaining walls, and broadens out downslope to the east. Where the cut took away the southern part of the Fieldstone House, it is 5.20 m wide.

It is noteworthy that the floor of the Fieldstone House, which is about the same level as the general floor of the KKT-F upper, western terrace, is about 80 cm higher than the level of the Ramp where it passes on the south on its east-west slope. The AIC took away precisely the place where the higher floor levels of the KKT-F and Fieldstone House stepped down to the Ramp.

One piece of evidence is the remnant of the northern wall of the Ramp, which exists on the west in a short stretch before the Cut took away the rest of it (figs. 23, 24). This wall is formed of the crushed limestone quarry debris that composes the upper terrace of the KKT-F. The wall is raised only slightly above the floor level formed in the same debris to the north, but steps down to the lower surface of the Ramp. Only traces remain of the silty mudbrick material that must have completed the wall over the shoulder of this core of limestone debris. The builders must have left this core as they formed the lower, sloping surface of the Ramp by cutting down and terracing the quarry debris just as they did in "Dan's Cut," the interface between the upper and lower terraces in the KKT-F (see above).

The AIC meanders down the slope from Water Tank 2 to the east where it took out the northern shoulder of the Ramp and cut right through the upper KKT-F terrace and the Fieldstone House. The AIC is filled with sandy limestone gravel markedly different than the crushed limestone quarry debris that formed the upper terrace of the KKT-F. The material is composed of much more sand, and the limestone fragments are smaller chips, more homogeneous in size, with sharper edges.

The sandier limestone gravel forms a bank of fill, 3.10 m wide, where the Cut broadens to 5.10 m south of the Fieldstone House. We have not determined if the limestone gravel banks up against the edge of the Cut where it took out the Fieldstone House and the quarry debris of the upper terrace, or whether the limestone gravel passes under the terrace, as a sandier, more gravelly layer that constitutes the upper terrace. We think it is more likely that the limestone gravel banks against the northern side of the cut, and this raises the question of whether people dumped this material into the cut to fill and patch it, which would in turn suggest that flowing water, perhaps from wadi flooding, made the cut during the time people occupied the KKT-F and the settlement within the GIII.VT.

This last hypothesis might fit with Reisner's (1931) observation that the GIII.VT in its first phase was damaged to a point of dysfunction by a violent wadi flood, after which people rebuilt the temple in the 6th Dynasty. Reisner thought the flash flood flowed down the northern side of the Menkaure causeway and breached the back, western wall of the GIII.VT. In the second phase people added thick fieldstone walls to the base of the western and northern sides of the temple as protection, Reisner thought, against damage from another such violent flow. In fact the AIC begins on its upper west end about on line with, maybe slightly north of, the path that Reisner projected for the damaging flash flood. Water Tank 2 might be located where it is in order to serve as a catchment and reservoir for such flood water, which, if it overflowed the brim of the tank, or was too powerful to be retained, might have flowed farther downslope washing out the KKT-F upper terrace, the Fieldstone House, and the northern side of the Ramp.

The Northeast Corner of the GIII.VT Exposed!

In the northeast corner of the Menkaure Valley Temple, Ana Tavares supervised the removal of sand that had accumulated since Selim Hassan's excavations. Here a large hole [29,810] (NEH) cuts through the Ramp surface and gives a section of its fill (see above, figs. 16, 25). Tavares supervised the emptying out of this circular hole of post-1932 sand with modern inclusions and recorded the important evidence given by its vertical section through the architecture and deposits.

Hassan seems to have understood this hole as a well, perhaps because it descended to the water table already when his forces cleared it out. Tavares emptied the semi-circular hole, which measures 5.60 to 5.80 m across, for a depth of 4.30 m and found the water at 15.40 m above sea level (asl). The water wicked up to a higher level through the section she cut in the post-1932 sandy fill. The initial reading, before this wicking up, compares with the level of the ground water in front of the Khafre Valley Temple during our 2008 season, and is about the same as the level Mark Lehner measured at points around the Sphinx in 1981 (Wetterstrom and Tavares 2008). It is our hypothesis, however, that this hole is not a purposeful well, but one of the exploratory pits such as George Reisner found around the GIII.VT already when he excavated in 1908, thinking they were made by "Arab treasure hunters" (Reisner 1931: 35).

Those who dug the NEH hole cut through the Ramp and its foundation/fill of limestone debris. They also took away the mudbrick casing on the northeast corner of the GIII.VT thereby exposing the temple foundation composed of six massive limestone blocks (fig. 25).

These core blocks are stacked in three courses. We set our GPMP survey point GIII.1 into the top of the upper core block in 1984 when it was flush with the ground. This block measures 5.08 m long, 1.45 m wide, and 1.70 m high. Our surveyors found themselves on a pedestal higher and higher as Tavares's team cleared out the NEH (fig. 26). The next block down is 1.60 m high.

These huge core blocks make it certain that Menkaure intended a colossal stone valley temple, like that of his predecessor, Khafre, to the northeast. As Reisner (1931) noted, the plan was not completed, and the evidence is that the next pharaoh, Shepseskaf, completed the temple in mudbrick. The NEH cut through the mudbrick casing, 1.30 m thick on the eastern temple wall, and 65 cm thick against the north side of the upper large core block.

We excavated down to the water table at 15.40 m asl but did not reach bedrock. The elevation on the top of the lowest core block, the third course down, is 16.24 m asl. We might compare this with the level at the bottom of the Glacis in front of the Ante-town, 16.00 m, or the level of the Old Kingdom terrace north of the gate in the Wall of the Crow, 16.30 m. One insight from this work is that the Ramp extends west along the northern side of the temple. As noted above, this was probably a building ramp, later resurfaced and used as a ceremonial road. It is possible

Figure 25. Ana Tavares cuts back the section through the post-1932 sand fill of the hole (NEH) at the northeast corner of the GIII. VT. The NEH cut the thick mudbrick casing on the northern and eastern faces of the huge limestone core blocks and the heavy limestone debris fill (on which Tavares stands) of the Ramp. Before the sand section collapsed, Tavares's emptying of the eastern half of the NEH descended to the water table and exposed the upper corner of a third, underlying, course of core blocks. View to the southwest.

Figure 26. Surveyor Azab Hassan rose higher and higher as we cleared the NEH hole deeper and deeper while each day he set up the Total Station on GPMP survey point GIII.1.

that the thick series of fieldstone walls or embankments surrounding Water Tank 2 reflect an effort to increase the height of the Ramp.

The results of this season modify our understanding of the GIII.VT. At the end of the use and occupation of the GIII.VT, the temple presented a blank eastern facade, dropping dramatically down to the east (the Glacis), flanked by two access roads leading up the desert to the west: on the south a covered causeway, leading to the southeast corner of the GIII.VT, around the southern side, and then up to the pyramid temple; on the north, the Ramp or broad roadway providing (the main?) ceremonial access to the Valley Temple, Water Tank 2, and the settlement of houses extramural to both the KKT and GIII.VT (see fig. 13). In the aspect of the double approach, we might compare the GIII.VT to the valley temples of Khafre and Pepi II, which had two access ramps. In the case of Pepi II, the ramps led to the two ends of the terrace fronting the temple (Lehner 1997: 26, 161). Some Egyptologists believe the valley temples are monumental forms of the "Purification Tent" (*ibw*) and "Mortuary Workshop" (*w3bt*) in the embalming and funeral rituals. Two ramps or roads lead to the Purification Tent and Mortuary Workshop in scenes from late Old Kingdom tomb chapels like those of Qar and Idu east of the Khufu Pyramid (Simpson 1976: figures 24, 35).

KKT-E: The Buried Building

In 2007 Lisa Yeomans cleared the surface sand for a width of 5.70 m east of the eastern KKT enclosure wall (Color Plate 1.1). She found that the bedrock drops vertically immediately under the eastern side of the eastern enclosure wall (fig. 27). She cleared this edge for a distance of 19 m north to south.

Yeomans next saw that the northern KKT enclosure wall continues eastward beyond the limits of the KKT as previously mapped (fig. 28). The wall is discernible as marl plaster lines in an unexcavated mass of toppled and "melted" mudbrick that for the most part remains unexcavated. The marl lines showed a doorway opening through the eastward continuation of the northern wall into a corridor that runs east-west, then turns south between the bedrock face under the earlier eastern limit of the town and the

Figure 27. View to the north along the eastern KKT enclosure wall. In 2007 Lisa Yeomans found the bedrock drops immediately along the eastern side of the wall (far right), which has been eroded down to the last few centimeters or to bedrock since Hassan's 1932 excavation.

thick western wall of a building lying on a lower level. This building extends farther east beneath the sand.

The lower lying building went undocumented by Hassan's mapmaker and possibly by subsequent missions whose members might have seen it. This building, and the extension of the northern enclosure wall, does not show in Hassan's published maps, nor does it show in the aerial photographs taken by the Royal Air Force from the Reisner Archives in the Boston Museum of Fine Arts (http://www.gizapyramids.org/code/emuseum.asp?newpage=visualsearch), taken four years after Hassan's excavations. The area east of the KKT "foot" appears to have been covered with clean sand.

KKT-E Goals in 2008

In 2007 Yeomans exposed the remains of a lower-lying mudbrick building in a trench 5.50 m wide (east of the bedrock edge) and 14 m long, north to south. At the end of that season she cleared another trench through the sandy overburden 10.70 m farther south and found the

Figure 28. The northern enclosure wall of the KKT, completely scoured down to bedrock along the KKT-N on the west, continued to the east beyond the corner with the eastern enclosure wall and beyond a bedrock edge. The foundation of the wall extends as a bedrock projection and marl-plastered mudbrick. View to the west.

Figure 29. Ana Tavares steps down into the southernmost of two trenches that Lisa Yeomans excavated through the sand to the lower-lying mudbrick building during 2007. View to the northwest.

continuation of the western mudbrick wall of the buried building (fig. 29).

In 2008 Mark Lehner and Kasia Olchowska supervised the removal of the sandy overburden between the northern and southern 2007 trenches. A principal goal was to find how the lower building related to the eastern end of the Khentkawes causeway. As far as we knew from the 2007 work, the causeway ends abruptly at the bedrock edge. In 2007 we ascertained that the causeway, 1.72 m wide, is a later entrance at this edge, replacing an earlier entrance into a corridor, 2.38 m wide, with a door that fitted into a large limestone pivot socket on the north, and a large jamb on the south (fig. 30). In either phase, how did people ascend from the floor level of the lower building up over the bedrock face to this eastern threshold of the Khentkawes Town?

In 2007 the area immediately east of the causeway threshold showed a mass of compact mud that banked up against the bedrock face, several centimeters below

the upper edge of the bedrock. Patches of silty soil that overlapped the more compact mudmass appeared to have been thrown up from a series of pits and shallow trenches from earlier, albeit modern, digging. In 2007 Yeomans and Collet had begun a shallow trench extending eastward, about on line with the causeway, with an eye to any evidence that a path continued eastward from the threshold of the Khentkawes causeway at or near the level of the top of the bedrock ledge.

The first task of an all-too-short 2008 season was to continue this trench to salvage any information about the path that led away to the east from the causeway threshold, and then sort out the sequence of the previous modern cuts and deposits (figs. 30, 31). This trench showed neither structural remains, nor layers that we could reasonably relate to the ancient access into the causeway, which ends abruptly at the bedrock drop. Finally, all we could hope for in the short season was to expose and map that part of the lower mudbrick building

Figure 30. Two-phase eastern entrance to the KKT. Kasia Olchowska adjusts a label board beside the large limestone pivot socket that functioned with a marl-plastered jamb on the south (lower right) to make an early-phase doorway, 2.38 m wide. The ancient builders narrowed this corridor to 1.72 m when they made the causeway, the southern line of which shows between the plaster line of the jamb and the pivot socket. The line immediately south of the pivot socket is the section through mudbrick collapse that Lisa Yeomans left from her 2007 excavation. View to the east.

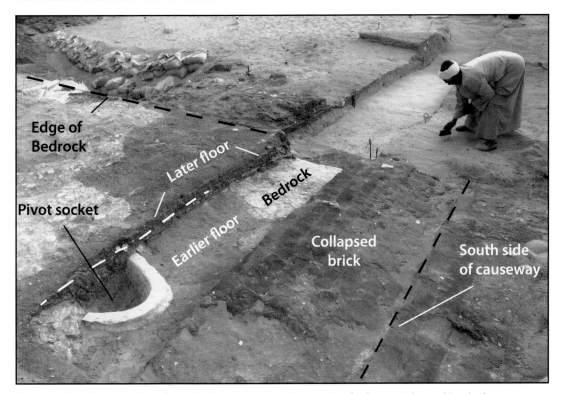

Figure 31. A shallow trench on line with the causeway and extending farther east shows thin silty layers cast up from previous modern digging overlying clean sand, with no evidence of a continuation of the causeway or an ancient path to the east beyond the bedrock edge. The large limestone threshold remains from a larger, wider entrance that predates the causeway and was covered by the floor when the causeway was in use. View to the northeast.

on line with the causeway between the northern and southern trenches of 2007.

Finding the Lower Terrace

Olchowska's careful excavation of all the deposits and recording of all the "cuts" (trenches and pits from previous excavations) helped us reconstruct the following scenario of how Selim Hassan's workers found the mudmass of the lower-lying building and how they recognized and traced its walls, making it all the more of a wonder why this extension of the Khentkawes Town went completely unmapped. In fact, the evidence suggests either that Hassan returned to KKT-E sometime after 1932, or that another mission, later than Hassan's, also worked along the eastern limit of the KKT as we know it from Hassan's map.

As they cleared the eastern boundary wall of the KKT, Hassan's workers must have first seen the bedrock edge running exactly flush with the eastern side of that wall (fig. 27). They began to move southwards along the bedrock edge, passing the opening of the causeway, digging narrow, shallow trenches, 40 to 60 cm wide, and a few centimeters to half a meter deep, into the top of a lower-founded mudmass that banked against the bedrock

face, probably to investigate how far the bedrock edge continued (fig. 32).

They realized that the mudmass must signal a lower building. We saw in 2007 where someone found the mudmass sloping down to the east and south from the northeast corner of the KKT. Glen Dash (2007) picked up this slope in his radar survey and suggested the possibility of a ramp. Excavators (Selim Hassan's?) cut into the mudmass and found the marl lines of the thick walls forming the northwest corner of the buried building, the corridor between its western wall and the bedrock face, and an entrance into the building (fig. 33). They saw these features, but left most of the "melted" mudbrick tumble filling the building.

About 6 m north of the causeway, Hassan's crew sunk a trench, 75 cm to 1 m wide, down along the bedrock face to find its depth (fig. 32). They cut through the western wall [29,050] of the buried building down to its lowest courses of mudbrick. They moved 2.5 m farther south, still north of the causeway by a little more than 2 m, and started another such trench, then plunged a deep hole [29,867], determined to find the bedrock floor (see page 40). When Olchowska cleared the backfill of this hole between April 8 and 10, we too found the bedrock floor at elevation

Figure 32. View to the north along the bedrock drop. The worker in the upper left corner cleans the scant remains of the KKT eastern enclosure wall. Selim Hassan's workers left narrow shallow trenches along the face of the bedrock edge as they tracked the run to the south of the edge and the underlying mudmass. They cut down into the mudmass to find the marl lines marking the northeast corner of the building (background), then they sunk a trench across the western wall of the buried building (ending at the worker with the dustpan).

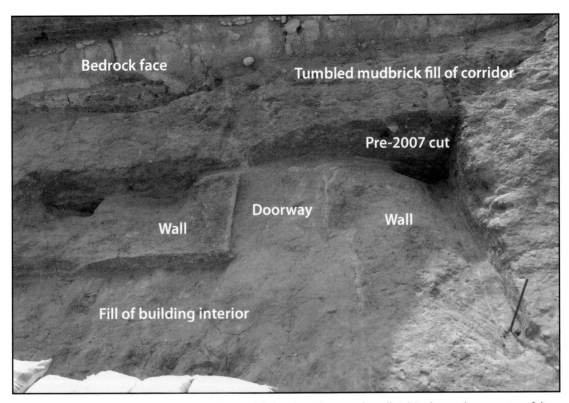

Figure 33. Pre-2007 excavators cut through the tumbled and amalgamated mudbrick in the northeast corner of the buried building. Their cut revealed the marl plaster lines of the western and northern walls of the building, with an entrance. The taller-standing mud is actually the remains of the mudbrick that collapsed from the walls and filled a corridor between the western wall and the bedrock face. After this collapse, forces of erosion scoured the ruins into a mass with a radical slope down to the east-southeast. View to the west.

Figure 34. Crusty brown, compact sand with multiple surface lines and scattered limestone chips that filled the southern part of Area KKT-E, derived from silt and limestone chips from erosion of the KKT mudbrick walls and quarry faces to the west-northwest. Soft, clean, wind-blown sand shows underneath.

16.53 m asl. With an elevation of the bedrock edge at the causeway threshold of 18.44 m, we have a vertical drop to a lower bedrock terrace of nearly 2 m. This discovery only increased the mystery of how one ascended from the lower terrace, or the floor of the buried building, up to the beginning of the causeway.

Two Missions Before?

Selim Hassan's men continued to trench farther south of the causeway to find the extent of the bedrock face, which decreases in height because the bedrock dips in this direction, and to track the buried building. But their work obviously stopped, and the sand drifted in, before their findings east of the KKT received enough attention to enter the cartographic and published record. We see indications that either Hassan's team, or that of another mission, returned to this area, KKT-E, before we began our work.

When Yeomans cleared east of the KKT, the sand to the north was soft and clean, but the sand to the south was very compact, tinted brown, with many scattered limestone chips (fig. 34). The surface of both sandy layers slopes, like the bedrock underneath, from north-northwest to south-southeast, a dip toward the wadi between the Moqattam and Maadi limestone formation outcrops at Giza. This brown crusty sand is a mixture of wind-blown sand and silt eroded off the KKT mudbrick walls after Hassan's excavation. The scattered limestone chips derive from the erosion of the quarry faces and rock-cut tombs to the northwest. The prevailing northwest wind blew this material into the deeper area down the slope to the southeast.

Except for her deep trenches, Yeomans leveled off her clearing of the sand slightly lower than the quarry edge on which runs the eastern wall of the KKT. For one reason, just at this level in our square 201.D36 her clearing exposed a plaster patch [29,856], about 30 × 30 cm, in which a wooden stake had been set with a thin nail or pin—clearly someone's survey marker at elevation 18.12 m asl (fig. 36). In 2007 we located a series of similar markers across the top of the mound of quarry debris that rises between the GIII.VT and KKT leg. As we mapped these markers, we assumed they were Selim Hassan's grid points of 1931–1932 (fig. 35).

Yeomans's deep southern trench (fig. 29) was almost exactly along the lines of at least two earlier trenches, dug through the sandy overburden by people who, like Yeomans, were investigating the mudmass and mudbrick wall underneath. In the south-facing section of her trench we could see the cut lines and fill of the previous two trenches. Someone, probably from Selim Hassan' crew, dug the earliest of these through clean sand. Someone else excavated the later trench, almost but not quite along the

same lines, after the brown crusty sand had accumulated in a layer 25-cm thick (the evidence being that they had to cut through this layer which had accumulated in the interval between the two excavations). Big brick-like chunks of this compacted combination of KKT silt and sand had fallen into the trench when it was backfilled after the second excavation. Yeomans's 2007 clearing left a thin layer of the same material over the cut lines of the second trench. The plaster, wood, and nail survey marker, survey point no. 13721 (fig. 35) had been set at this level, after only a little bit more of a layer of the crusty material had accumulated. If Selim Hassan's men dug the first trench, who excavated the second trench before Yeomans dug the third trench along this same line?

We cleared the brown crusty sand in the lower southern part of Area KKT-E (about 15 m east-west × 30 m) in several passes, roughly corresponding to surfaces that had remained exposed for some time (fig. 34). It was only after we cleared all the brown crusty sand down to the surface of the underlying, softer, clean sand that we exposed the southernmost of a series of gray cement supports for iron posts. The cement supports of this series in the north were exposed before we excavated the brown crusty sand because the clean sand rose high there, and remained unencumbered with the brown crusty sand. But the southern cement post bases were several centimeters lower than the plaster and wood survey marker, which the brown crusty sand had buried. We imagine that these cement bases were for the wire fence erected east of the KKT excavations shortly after or during Hassan's 1931–1932 excavations.

Again, it appears either that Selim Hassan's crew returned for more investigative digging in a later season, or the crew of a later mission probed through the sandy overburden to investigate the ruins of the buried building, a mission that intended a wide survey over the greater site, as witnessed by the survey markers over the central mound of quarry debris (figs. 35, 36). It may be that the former explanation is correct, for this fits with other evidence that Hassan's map of the Khentkawes monument, the KKT, and the GIII.VT, which has formed the basic template and record of the site for Egyptologists, was surveyed late, some years after his excavation was concluded. We know that Selim Hassan's mission continued at Giza through 1938, six years after he discovered the KKT. We have even speculated that the map was based to some extent on the Royal Air Force (RAF) aerial photograph of the Giza Necropolis that is part of the MFA Reisner Archive (http://www.gizapyramids.org/code/emuseum. asp?newpage=visualsearch). The aerial photography was taken in 1936, four years after Selim Hassan's team excavated KKT. This might explain why we have found a few of the plaster and wood survey markers on mudbrick

Figure 35. A survey assistant holds the reflector pole on point 13721, a metal pin set in a wooden stake in a plaster base. Someone from a previous archaeological project set the survey point after crusty sand formed over the top of the fill of a trench, showing in the south-facing section of Lisa Yeomans's southern 2007 trench. The trench had been excavated twice, as indicated by two cut lines. Yeomans's was the third trench to follow the mud bank that resulted from the collapse of the building along the bedrock face. View to the north.

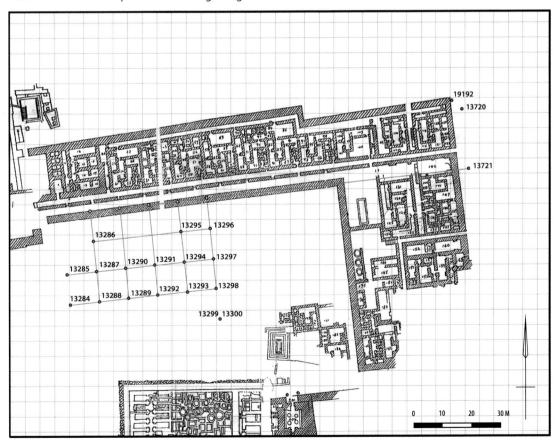

Figure 36. Map of points marked by pins in wooden stakes set in plaster. Point 13721 (far right) was founded on the brown, crusty sand that fills the southern part of Area KKT-E. Drawing after Hassan fig. 2, geo-referenced by C. Mazzucato.

ruins that must have badly eroded since they were first exposed in 1932. A mapping of the KKT much later than the conclusion of its 1932 excavation might also explain why the buried building, while probed and certainly known, never made it into the map. Drift sand had rapidly filled the probe trenches by the time the RAF photos were taken, and maybe by the time ground survey was done for the map that Selim Hassan published. We should note that the plaster and wood survey markers comprise a grid that does not match that of Selim Hassan's map of the Central Field (see large color fold-out in Hassan 1943).

Stairway to Heaven?

Once Olchowska worked through the spoil heaps, patches, and pits from previous digging, and after we excavated all the brown crusty sand deposited after 1932, the team moved deeper along the steeply sloping face of the mudmass directly east of the Khentkawes causeway by removing sand with mud spots that had no doubt been cast back into a trench that workers dug previously in the same place and for the same purpose (fig. 37). This bank contained articulated mudbrick, tumbled mudbrick, and crushed limestone debris that extended out 2.25 m from

the bedrock face and descended from 18.44 m asl at the end of the causeway threshold to 17.18 m. Whatever structure was embedded in this material had eroded into a steep slope of about 30°.

That structure began to announce itself as we descended. A roughly vertical marl plaster line against articulated (as opposed to tumbled out of place) mudbricks appeared to be the northern wall of a structure (fig. 38). The plastered bricks lean in to the south with a pronounced slope or batter like a retaining wall. The western wall of the buried building that Yeomans found in 2007 butted up against the battered face. At first we began to think of a steep stairway straight up from east to west to the threshold of the causeway, a stairway to the "Doors of Heaven," as the pyramid valley temples might have been known according to an article by Egyptologist Edward Brovarski (1977). But if this battered wall on the north framed a stairway up to the causeway we could not find the corresponding frame-wall on the south.

Instead we could see a nearly continuous band of white limestone debris on a gradual slope down to the south through the dark bank of the mudmass (figs. 38, 39). Our Eureka moment came when we realized this whitish

Figure 37. Kasia Olchowska points to the section of a deep pit that she cleared of post-1932 fill. Selim Hassan's workers dug the pit to find the bottom of the bedrock edge and floor of the lower terrace on which the buried building was founded. The workers remove clean sand with mud spots from in front of the causeway threshold. View to the south.

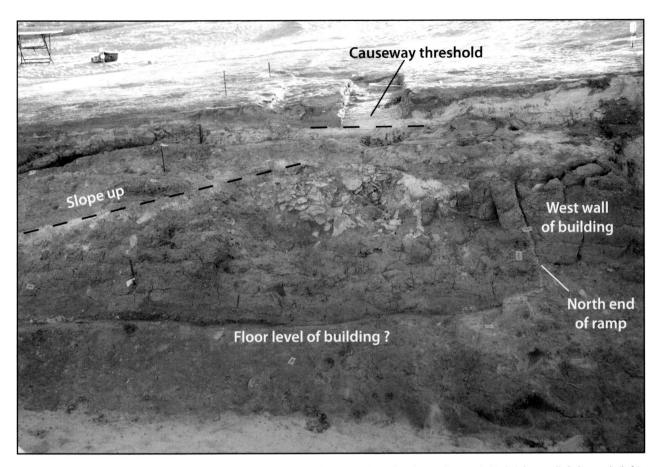

Figure 38. The ramp in the mud bank. The nearly vertical line of plastered mudbricks on the north (right), leans slightly south (left), marking the end of the ramp, which rises on a bed of limestone debris (left) sloping to a high point at the threshold of the causeway. The western wall of the lower building abuts the northern end of the ramp. A patch of marl plaster marks the floor level of the building, which was mostly removed when some force cut down through the mud foundation. View to the west.

debris was the fill of a ramp that ascended to the causeway threshold from the south against the bedrock face. Now, in the shallow cuts that Hassan's workers made along the bedrock ledge, we could see the top of this limestone debris fill. One entered the causeway by ascending from south to north on this ramp, then turning west 90° to cross the causeway threshold.

There might be in this sloped, deteriorated mass, the possibility of a straight-on stairway to the causeway. If so, it is very steep, but steep stairways are not usual in ancient Egyptian architecture. At the base of the northern retaining wall—the battered line of plastered mudbrick—we came upon a patch of marl floor, only 40 cm wide, which appears to be the bottom of the ramp, and possibly the floor of the buried building. The elevation of this patch is 17.18 m asl. We know from the 1932 trenches that the lower bedrock terrace is at elevation 16.60 m asl. The 58 cm difference is taken up by a layer of dense silt with toppled mudbrick, which has been cut through. It looks as though the floor was robbed and this, a foundation layer, was cut through. If this is a foundation layer, the buried building

was a rebuild of some earlier structure, indicated by the toppled bricks.

We mapped articulated bricks for some distance to the south along the lower, outer, eastern edge of the bank of mud and limestone debris (figs. 39, 40). These brick courses must belong to the base of an outside wall that retained the limestone debris fill of the ascending ramp. The outside wall probably rose some distance above the sloping floor of the ramp. When erosion made a 30° cut through the rectilinear cross-section of the ramp, it left the limestone debris showing on its rise through the core of the ramp.

We did not continue clearing the sand east of the stairway-ramp down to expose the bedrock terrace because we were at the end of our season. We were intrigued to find, just where we stopped, a common bread pot of a style quite different than the thousands of bread pots from the HeG settlement and bakeries south of the Wall of the Crow, but very common at the end of the Old Kingdom, some 300 years after the 4th Dynasty (fig. 41).

Figure 39. Kasia Olchowska maps the ramp in Area KKT-E. Her north-south datum measuring tape crosses the line of the outer wall of the ramp, of which traces show on the lower left. View to the west.

Figure 40. Kasia Olchowska maps the ramp in Area KKT-E. Her north-south datum measuring tape crosses the line of the outer wall of the ramp. The ramp, like the rest of the KKT layout, and in contrast to the GIII.VT, is oriented slightly west of north, like Heit el-Ghurab, the settlement south of the Wall of the Crow. View to the north.

Valley Approach

Our discovery of another ramp in front of the Khentkawes causeway, plus the broader Ramp at the GIII.VT-KKT interface, draws our attention to the overall access into the whole complex and into the Giza Necropolis as a whole. If we project the lines of both ramps downslope, they point to the southeast part of the KKT, which is at the bottom of the general bedrock dip into the central wadi between the Moqattam and Maadi formation outcrops at Giza (fig. 42). It is just this part of the settlement, the southeast corner of the KKT, which was unobtainable already in 1932 because of the proximity of the modern cemetery. Hence the approach from the southeast is missing from Hassan's map. In our next season we hope to gain a little more of this low corner.

We will also begin to excavate into the buried building in KKT-E (fig. 43). Is it in fact a discrete building, or just an enclosure around a broad open reception area? In Hassan's map the eastern wall of the foot of the town (KKT-F) shows a turn to the east, about 35 m south of the causeway threshold. The turn hints that the whole foot of the KKT might have turned to the east and continued in that direction (for a width of about 30 m, fig. 42). The distance from this turn to the extension eastward of the northern KKT enclosure wall measures 52 m, 100 ancient Egyptian royal cubits. The two walls would contain a rectangular space 100 cubits wide. The Valley Temple of Menkaure (GIII.VT) is a little shy of 52 m wide, so it would fit into the projected space below the Khentkawes causeway. We know from what we have cleared so far that the buried building is at least 30 m wide, north to south (fig. 42). If it is a discrete building, it is most likely the true valley temple of Khentkawes, possibly of a size equal to that of Menkaure.

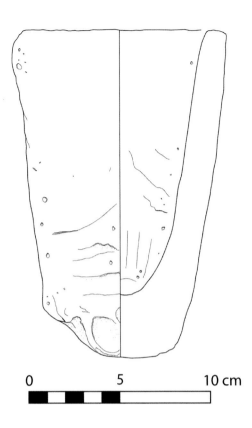

0   5   10 cm

1:2

Figure 41. Bread mold found during clearance of sand east of the stairway-ramp down in KKT-E. Drawing by Edyta Klimaszewska-Drabot and Aleksandra Księżak.

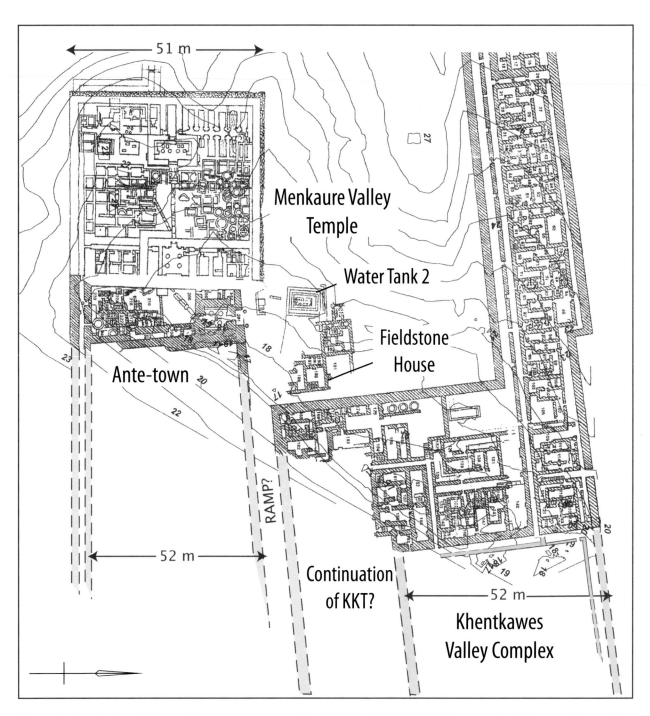

Figure 42. A projection of the possible arrangement east of the GIII.VT and KKT. The GIII.VT, measured off the geo-referenced 1:1,000 map, is 51 m wide, north to south. The angle of the northern Ante-town would place its northern face 52 m (100 cubits) from the northern wall of the GIII.VT causeway if both walls are projected about 50 m east, roughly parallel to the southern wall of the KKT foot. Hassan's map of the eastern KKT enclosure wall shows a turn to the east. If projected, the distance from the northern face of this wall is 52 m from the northern face of the eastward extension of the northern enclosure wall of the KKT. The GIII.VT would fit within this space, which contains what remains of a mudbrick building, possibly the Valley Temple of Queen Khentkawes. Drawing after Hassan fig. 2, georeferenced by C. Mazzucato.

Figure 43. The western and northern sides of the buried building partially cleared, with the Sphinx and Great Pyramid of Khufu in the background. View to the north.

References

Abd el-Aziz, A.

2007   Main Street Excavations. In *Giza Reports, The Giza Plateau Mapping Project, Vol. 1: Project History and Survey, Main Street, Gallery III.4, and Ceramics*, edited by M. Lehner and W. Wetterstrom, 109–161. Boston: Ancient Egypt Research Associates, Inc.

Brovarski, E.

1977   The Doors of Heaven. *Orientalia Nova Series* 46: 107–115.

Dash, G.

2007   A Report of the 2006 Geophysical Season at Giza: A Ground-Penetrating Radar Study. Feb. 24. Report on file, Ancient Egypt Research Associates, Inc.

2009   2006 Geophysical Season at Giza: A Ground-Penetrating Radar Study. In *Giza Plateau Mapping Project Seasons 2006–2007 Preliminary Report*, Giza Occasional Papers 3 (*GOP3*), by M. Lehner, M. Kamel, and A. Tavares, 153–158. Boston, MA: Ancient Egypt Research Associates, Inc.

Fairman, A.

2008   Summary for Archives, KKT-AI excavations 2008. July 21. Report on file, Ancient Egypt Research Associates, Inc.

Hassan, S.

1943   *Excavations at Giza. Vol. IV.* 1932–1933. Cairo: Government Press.

Kawae, Y.

2007   Mapping Khentkawes. *AERAGRAM* 8.2: 10–12. Boston, MA: Ancient Egypt Research Associates, Inc.

2009a   Giza Laser Scanning Survey 2006. In *GOP3*: 166–175.

2009b   House Unit 1 (SFW.H1): Interim Report. In *GOP3*: 88–91.

Kemp, B.

1983   Old Kingdom, Middle Kingdom and Second Intermediate Period c. 2686–1552 BC. In *Ancient Egypt*, edited by B. G. Trigger, B. J. Kemp. D. O'Connor, and A. B. Lloyd, 71–182. Cambridge: Cambridge University Press.

1989   *Ancient Egypt: Anatomy of a Civilization.* London: Routledge.

2006   *Ancient Egypt: Anatomy of a Civilization*, 2nd edition. London: Routledge.

Lehner, M.

1997   *The Complete Pyramids.* New York: Thames and Hudson.

Lehner, M., M. Kamel, and A. Tavares

2006   *Giza Plateau Mapping Project Season 2005 Preliminary Report*, Giza Occasional Papers 2, Cairo: Ancient Egypt Research Associates, Inc.

Reisner, G. A.

1931   *Mycerinus, the Temples of the Third Pyramid at Giza.* Cambridge, MA: Harvard University Press.

Simpson, W. K.

1976   *The Mastabas of Qar and Idu, G 7101 and 7102.* Giza Mastabas 2. Boston, MA: Museum of Fine Arts.

Wetterstrom, W., and A. Tavares

2008   Lost City Site, Flooded! *AERAGRAM* 9.1: 5–6. Boston, MA: Ancient Egypt Research Associates, Inc.

Yeomans, L.

2007   Data Structure Report for the 2007 Season at Khentkawes (KKT). Report on file, Ancient Egypt Research Associates, Inc.

Archaeological Science 2008

by Mary Anne Murray

The Giza Field Laboratory, under the direction of Dr. Mary Anne Murray, hosted the first full season of our new Archaeological Science program from March 1 to May 31, 2008. The core of the program is an interdisciplinary, international team of 38 specialists from 10 countries[1] who analyze the material culture and environmental evidence from the AERA excavations, including the ceramics, artifacts, human bone, animal bone, plants, mud sealings, chipped stone, pigments, wood charcoal, roofing material and mudbrick, as well as faience and the probable by-products of faience production. In addition, this season a team of material scientists from Japan carried out the chemical and elemental analysis of several classes of material culture using X-ray diffraction and X-ray fluorescence (XRD/XRF). We also have an experienced team of photographers, illustrators, and a videographer to document various aspects of the analysis and results.[2]

The metamorphosis of our building, the Lab itself—nestled as it is between the Giza pyramids—from a simple storeroom of excavated material to a vital working laboratory has been a gradual process. The Lab is much larger than you would imagine from the exterior, with six rooms containing the archaeological traces from 20 years of AERA excavations at Giza. In each room, all of the floor to ceiling units and shelves are numbered and mapped with the details of their contents and of their origin—the nearby settlements of the Giza pyramid builders, Heit el Ghurab (HeG), and the Khentkawes town (KKT).

During this first major Archaeological Science session in the Giza Field Laboratory, we strongly encouraged collaboration between the specialists to achieve a compre-

hensive, integrated, and holistic narrative of daily life in an ancient Egyptian settlement. The ultimate goal of our program of excavation and specialist analysis is the final publication of our integrated results. Toward this end, the specialists worked on materials from two areas of the site that will be fully published in our monograph series, *Giza Reports*, in the next two years: the Royal Administrative Building (RAB) and Area AA.

During the 2008 season, all specialists focused on completing the analysis of their data from the RAB, an important component of the HeG settlement. By pooling and integrating data, each specialist can contribute to understanding the area's complexity, which includes a multi-phased series of buildings and rooms on the west side of a large complex.

Face-to-face meetings, as well as successive Skype sessions between Boston; London; Warsaw; Cairo; Nice; Berlin; and Ann Arbor, Michigan, facilitated integration. The process culminated in a day-long RAB Workshop in April 2009 to discuss the final results prior to publication. Excavator and specialists had the opportunity to review every step on the long and gradual path towards publication of a well-integrated final excavation report. This painstaking approach offers an informed interpretation of the daily life of a particular settlement more than the use of any single source of evidence alone.

We will carry out the same process for our publication of Area AA, which includes the Pedestal Building, a large structure enclosed in thick walls with two rows of enigmatic pedestals, possibly used for storage. The specialists are following the same protocol for material from the nearby site of Khentkawes Town (KKT).

The 2008 Archaeological Science program laid the practical and theoretical ground work of a more comprehensive research agenda for future seasons. Additional scientists and other specialists will join our team in the Giza Field Lab, including well known experts in the study of ground stone tools, fresh and salt water shells, plaster and mortar, geology and minerals, and plant phytoliths—

---

1.   America, Egypt, Sweden, Poland, Portugal, Britain, Japan, Thailand, Serbia, and Germany.

2.   Our work at the Giza Field Lab is greatly facilitated by our Supreme Council of Antiquities inspector Ahmed Ezz and our team of experienced workmen, some of whom have worked with us for many years: Mohammed Hassan, Abd el Latif, Said Salah, Ashraf Hassan, Alaa Mohammed, and Ahmed Sindewa.

the silica skeletons of plants, which provide a wealth of environmental information.

Another fundamental facet of the Archaeological Science program is the specialist element of our Field School teaching which takes place in our Lab. Here, the Egyptian SCA Inspectors learn about ceramics, human bone, animal bone, plants, lithics, conservation, and illustration. This program has been very successful in providing Egyptian archaeologists with specialist vocational skills which, in the past, have been normally provided by foreign missions to Egypt.

In the following article from the Giza Lab, Jessica Kaiser outlines the osteological results from the Khentkawes (KKT) skeletons. Her excavation team includes several members of the Supreme Council of Antiquities who were former students of the AERA Field School and who are now Field School teachers and remain an important part of both our AERA field and lab teams.

2008 KKT Human Osteology

by Jessica Kaiser

The first two burials were uncovered in the Khentkawes Town (KKT) area during the 2005 season. However because the 2005 Field School was taking up much of the field resources at the time and because no actual excavation took place in KKT in 2005, they were left for a later season. In the 2008 excavation season, several more burial cuts were recognized in the KKT-F and KKT-AI areas, and nine burials (#452–460) were eventually excavated during March and April (Color Plates 1 and 2.1). The orientation of these burials was generally north-south with the heads located in the north end of the burials. Three of these were found oriented slightly off north; one oriented 10° west of magnetic north, a double burial oriented 20° east of magnetic north and one 15° east of magnetic north (Burials 456, 457, and 458, respectively). Several of the burials had been truncated and were incomplete, but judging from the burials that were generally complete, the bodies were positioned on their backs with their legs extended, thus indicating a late Old Kingdom or later burial. This corresponds to the burials cutting into the Old Kingdom features or walls. The remaining burials were incomplete with indications of having previously been excavated or truncated.

Team Members

Jessica Kaiser (University of California, Berkeley) led the 2008 Osteological team, and team members included Johnny Karlsson (Stockholm Historical Museum), Afaf Wahba Abd-el-Salam (Egypt's Supreme Council of Antiquities), Amanda Agnew (Ohio State University), Brianne Daniels (University of California, Berkeley), Ahmed Gabr (Supreme Council of Antiquities) and Sandra Koch (United States Federal Bureau of Investigation)[3].

Aims and Objectives

In terms of the larger Ancient Egypt Research Associates (AERA) project, the aims of the cemetery excavations on

---

3. Kaiser Archaeological Services keeps the original documentation of excavation and analysis in Livermore, California. Copies of the documentation are kept in AERA archives in both Giza and Boston.

---

the plateau have always been to scientifically remove and record the human burials overlying the Old Kingdom archaeology that is the main focus of the AERA excavations. In terms of mortuary archaeology, the skeletal assessment aims to determine age, sex, and stature, as well as any pathological conditions from which the individuals may have suffered. In addition, the 2008 excavations gave the new additions to the team (Agnew, Daniels, and Koch) an opportunity to familiarize themselves with the AERA recording and excavation procedures, in preparation for future field school seasons when they themselves may be teachers. Information was also sought regarding the date of the KKT burials.

Methodology

As is general practice at AERA projects, bone specialists excavated all human remains. This is necessary due to the poor preservation of the bone. Without the expertise of a bone specialist, information would be lost. Further, and also according to AERA procedure, a large part of the skeletal analysis was carried out in situ, due to the fragmentary nature of the remains. In many cases, only bone stains remain, and measurements have to be taken before lifting the skeletal elements. The excavation procedure follows the guidelines set forth in the MOLAS manual (Museum of London 1994), while the skeletal recording system is site-specific, but largely adapted from Standards (Buikstra and Ubelaker 1994). All of the burials were photographed, elevations recorded by a total station system, and the skeletal remains were drawn with a computer mapping program, the resulting files to be imported into the overall plans of the site.

All burials from KKT will be analyzed in detail in the laboratory, including assessing the preservation and completeness of each skeleton, as well as determining the age, sex, and stature of the individuals, and any pathological conditions.

Osteological Analysis

Osteological analysis centers on the determination of a demographic profile of the assemblage studied, based on the assessment of sex, age, and stature, as well as measurements and non-metric traits. This information is crucial in order to determine the occurrence of disease types and age-related changes. It is also decisive for identifying gender dimorphism in occupation, lifestyle, and diet, as well as the role of different age groups in society.

Preservation

No single factor determines the preservation of skeletal remains. Differential preservation may occur between individuals of different sex, age, and size, as well as between bones of varying density from the same individual. Burial environment and disposition of the remains (Roksandic 2002), incomplete excavation and post-depositional disturbance, as well as excavation and post-excavation loss of skeletal material (Ubelaker 1978: 177) can also influence bone condition. At AERA, we calculate a preservation score for each burial by scoring 7 paired standard measurements for sub-adults and 18 paired and 5 unpaired for measurements for adults, as well as presence or absence of 5 paired and 6 unpaired selected skeletal landmarks for sub-adults and 8 paired and 5 unpaired skeletal landmarks for adults. Paired measurements are ones taken on bones that occur on both the left and right side of the body, such as the long bones; femur and humerus for example. Unpaired bones are those of which the human body only contains one, such as the sacrum or the occipital. The total for each skeleton is divided by the highest obtainable score, so that a perfectly preserved skeleton will have a taphonomy score of one, and any missing values would result in a total of less than one.

The preservation of the KKT burials was generally very poor, due to the fact that several of the burials had been truncated, most likely by the Selim Hassan excavations in the 1930s, and that the area was left open after the excavations concluded. All of the burials were extremely fragmentary, and in several of the cuts only a small percentage of the skeleton remained. Further, two of the more intact burials were covered with layers of heavy limestone blocks, which crushed the underlying bones. The taphonomy score of the first three burials excavated in March averaged 0.03, substantially below the 0.16 which is the lowest recorded score from the HeG site south of the Wall of the Crow. The taphonomy score for the six burials excavated in April is awaiting final analysis in the storeroom, but is also expected to be very low.

Minimum Number of Individuals

As standard procedure, a count of the "minimum number of individuals" (MNI) is carried out on all material excavated at AERA in order to establish how many individuals are represented by the articulated and disarticulated human bones recovered during excavation. The MNI is calculated by counting duplicates of identified and sided skeletal elements. The provisional MNI of the KKT burials from 2008 was 10, but this number may have to be amended once final analysis has been carried out for all burials.

Age Assessment

Bones and teeth form and grow in relatively predictable patterns up until approximately 25 years of age, when the skeleton is completely formed. Following complete formation of the skeleton, degeneration of skeletal elements and dental wear can be utilized to assess the age of older individuals. Data from comparative materials of individuals of known ages are used for comparison (Brothwell 1981; Buikstra and Ubelaker 1994; Cox 2000; Ubelaker 1978; White and Folkens 2005). However, since degenerative changes tend to vary with lifestyle, occupation, and health of the individual, age assessment is more secure in younger individuals, and age-brackets tend to widen with advanced age.

The human dentition is constructed of dense, hard materials, relatively resistant to decay in the ground, and often outlasting bone. Consequently, the dentition plays an important role in the work of any anthropologist, especially when dealing with poorly preserved material. At AERA, we employed coding of dental-wear patterns according to Brothwell (1981) to assess the age-at-death of adult individuals, and eruption patterns according to Ubelaker (1978) for immature remains. Other methods used to determine age at death were as follows: age-related changes at the pubic symphysis according to Todd (1920; 1921) and Brooks and Suchey (1990), modal age-related changes to the auricular surface of the coxae according to Lovejoy et al. (1985), sternal-end ossification of the fourth rib according to İşcan et al. (1984), and progression of endosteal reabsorption of the cortex with concomitant expansion of the marrow cavity according to Acsádi and Nemeskéri (1970). The latter method is based on trabecular patterns and, as such, could only be used when the bone in question was already fragmentary since no radiographic equipment was available for use. Each criterion was then weighed in order to arrive at an age assessment for each individual. The sample was divided into age groups after Sjøvold (1978) in the following way:

Infant	0–1 years
Infans I	0–7 years
Infans II	5–14 years
Juvenilis	10–24 years
Adultus	18–44 years
Maturus	35–64 years
Senilis	50–79 years
Adult*	18–79 years

*(includes the groups Adultus, Maturus, and Senilis)

In addition, a narrower age-range was also given for each individual when possible. Both age group and age-range were noted on the burial forms, together with the criteria upon which the assessment was based.

Due to the fragmentary nature of the KKT assemblage, only one of the burials could be aged with precision. This was the young adult male (16–21 years of age). Two burials (459 and 460) were so fragmented that no age assessment was possible at all. Of the remaining seven burials, four were Adult (18–79), and three were Senilis (50+).

Sex Assessment

Within all human populations, growth changes during adolescence lead to distinctive dimorphic differences in the male and female skeleton. The hipbones present the most reliable indication of sex in the human skeleton, followed by the cranium. Sex determination was therefore first and foremost based on cranial and pelvic morphology. The indicators in Table 1 were used in the analysis.

All dimorphic features were scored according to *Standards* (Buikstra and Ubelaker 1994: 15–21) so that comparison with similar samples would be possible in the future. However, due to the poor level of preservation of the sample we could not always use all features listed above on each skeleton, but all observable traits were recorded for each individual. In addition, to complement the morphological analysis, a number of measurements were taken when obtainable. These were as follows:

Femur	Vertical diameter of caput
	Epicondylar width
	(After Krogman 1962)
Humerus	Vertical diameter of caput
	Transversal diameter of caput
	Epicondylar width
	(After Sjøvold 1978, based on
	measurements in Gejvall 1960)
Sternum	Length of the manubrium
	Length of the meso-sternum
	Width of the first sternebra
	Width of the third sternebra
	(Jit et al. 1980)

The results were then classified according to five different groups: Undetermined or Allophys (?), Female (F), Probable female (F?), Male (M), or Probable Male (M?). The KKT material included two male and three female individuals, and five individuals with such poor preservation that no sex assessment was attempted.

Metric Analysis

Final metric analysis is pending work in the laboratory, but preliminary stature could be calculated for the two least fragmented skeletons in Burial 457. The male in 457 was approximately 177.8 cm tall (between 173.6 to 182 cm with error margins taken into account), and the female was approximately 166.5 cm tall (162.8 to 170.1 cm with error margins taken into account). The remaining skeletons were too fragmentary to allow for any long-bone measurements from which to calculate stature.

Non-Metric Traits

Non-metric traits are additional sutures, facets, bony processes, canals and foramina that occur in a minority of skeletons and are thought to suggest diversity and familial affiliation between individuals (Saunders 1989). The only non-metric trait recorded in the KKT material was a divided hypoglossal canal in the male individual of Burial 457, Skeleton [30,211].

Pathological Analysis

The analysis of skeletal and dental manifestations of disease can provide a vital insight into the health and diet of past populations, as well as their living conditions and occupations. Three individuals (Skeleton [29,456], Burial 454, and Skeletons [30,210] and [30,211], Burial 457) exhibited skeletal manifestations of disease.

The majority of the recorded pathological lesions in the KKT material were arthritic. This is not surprising, given that arthritis is one of the three main causes of lesions in archaeological assemblages (Ortner and Putschar 1985: 545). All three individuals exhibited lesions on the spine (lipping and osteophytic growth). Vertebral osteoarthritis is directly attributable to spinal stress, and can be viewed as one of the costs of the fully erect bipedal posture of humans, in that we are more susceptible to spinal stress than quadrupedal vertebrates (Roberts and Manchester 1995: 105).

Studies of relatively modern skeletal samples have shown that osteophytic growth in the spine occurred in a large proportion of the individuals by the third decade of life, and in all individuals by age 50 (Nathan 1962). An individual engaged in hard physical labor is more likely to develop osteophytic growth of the spine than a sedentary worker, and thus the more active lifestyle in antiquity probably contributed to an earlier development of vertebral osteoarthritis (Roberts and Manchester 1995: 107). In skeletal materials from ancient Egypt, a pattern of osteoarthritis to the lower (lumbar) spine in men, and to the cervical spine in women is often observed. This has been interpreted as men engaging in more heavy lifting and hard manual labor, and women carrying heavy loads on their heads. It is interesting to note that the pattern in the KKT material is the opposite: the two cases of osteoarthritic changes to the lower spine occurred in the female individuals, while the male in Burial 457 had osteoarthritic changes to the cervical spine (Atlas and Axis).

In addition to the vertebral lipping, the older woman in Burial 457 also suffered from joint changes in her left hand, as well as healed Cribra Orbitalia and active Porotic Hyperostosis of the Parietals and Occipital bones (porosity of the orbital roofs and cranial bones, respectively). These two lesions are quite common in archaeological materials, and are usually attributed to iron deficiency anemia (Aufderheide and Rodriguez-Martin 1998: 348–350). The exact cause of the anemia is impossible to determine, but in women it is often thought to be connected to breast feeding or nutritional deficiencies. Because of the advanced age of the female in Burial 457, it is probably safe to assume that the latter is more likely to be the cause of her cranial lesions.

Dental Health

The dentition is the only feature of the human skeleton that directly interacts with the environment during life, providing archaeologists with information on health, stress and disease, diet, occupation, economy, and cultural behavior. Further, teeth are the hardest and the most indestructible of human tissues, and often outlast other skeletal elements in the archaeological record. Because of the post-depositional disturbance in KKT, however, teeth were only recovered from four individuals, Burial 454 and 455, and from the two individuals in Burial 457. In all four cases, the teeth recovered showed evidence of extensive dental attrition. Dental attrition is one of several degenerative changes associated with aging (Aufderheide and Rodriguez-Martin 1998: 398). Because of the excessive amount of grit in the foodstuffs of ancient Egyptians, dental attrition is often particularly pronounced in skeletal assemblages from Egypt (Leek 1972). The dental wear in the four cases from KKT ranged from 5+-7, according to the Brothwell scoring system, indicating an advanced age for all four individuals, even with the often greater wear in ancient Egyptians taken into account. In one case, the male in Burial 457, the attrition was so severe that it had caused osteoarthritic changes and eburnation to the temporo-mandibular joint (Hodges 1991). This individual also had a large interproximal cavity between the right mandibular second and third molars, with slight abscess formation at the apex of the tooth roots. In addition, this individual displayed extensive and highly uneven wear of all four upper incisors, as well as the left maxillary premolars, indicating that he may have used his teeth as tools during life. Both individuals in Burial 457 also showed signs of periodontal disease, with several teeth lost antemortem. In Burials 454 and 455, not enough remained of the alveolar bone to determine whether or not the individuals suffered from periodontal disease.

Finds

The preservation of the nine burials excavated in 2008 was poor; what was present was generally fragmentary or bone stains. Previous excavation by Selim Hassan or other post-burial cuts damaged the majority, with only three burials more complete (Burials 453, 454, and 457) but fragmented/eroded by the burial environment. Beads were found in five burials (Burials 454, 455, 457, 458, and 459). Pottery sherds consistent with the 6th Dynasty or earlier, and charcoal material were found in the fill of the majority of the burials, and this material was separated for further analysis. No apparent masks were found with these burials and the skeletal remains were fragmentary and/or incomplete.

Dating

All the burials excavated at KKT had been truncated to some extent, presumably by the Selim Hassan excavations, and none were preserved to their original depth. Thus, the original surface from which the burials were cut is lost to us. This, coupled with the fact that there were no intentional burial items in the graves that were strong chronological indicators, makes dating the remains very difficult. Pottery sherds and a small number of beads and fragments of mother-of-pearl were found in the burial fills, but not in immediate association with the bodies. Thus, these items could have been deposited accidentally in the burial fills during the infilling of the cuts at the time of burial. Two of the deeper burials contained a layer of limestone, similar to the Late Period burials south of the Wall of the Crow East at the HeG site. However, none of the pottery that came out of the burial fills was later than the 6th Dynasty (A. Wodzińska, personal communication, 2008). Of course, this may be due to abandonment of the area after the 6th Dynasty, and does not in itself mean that the burials date to this period, since none of the pottery sherds came from complete jars. In addition, there was no indication of the bodies having been tightly wrapped, as would be expected if they dated from the Late, Ptolemaic, or Roman Periods (the position of the skeletal elements in the burials at the HeG site often shows evidence of tight wrapping). Further, the north-south orientation of the burials is inconsistent with a Late Period or later date, as burials from these periods are usually oriented east-west. In lower status Old Kingdom burials, the bodies are typically in a tightly flexed position, though oriented north-south. The lack of grave goods and grave markers suggests that the KKT burials were not of high status, so the extended burial position is probably also inconsistent with an Old Kingdom date. There is ample evidence for a north-south extended position in Old Kingdom burials, but then it is usually in elite burials with a tomb, burial chamber, and sarcophagus (Ikram and Dodson 1998: 143). Consequently, it is possible that the burials in KKT date to the end of the Old Kingdom/First Intermediate period, but it is equally possible that they are much later. All that can be said with certainty, since the burial cuts truncate the Old Kingdom walls of the site, is that the KKT burials definitely post-date the KKT architecture.

Conclusion

Because of the small size of the KKT sample, it is difficult to draw any general conclusions as to the exact nature of the interments. Further, the poor preservation and lack of burial goods make dating difficult. However, the fact that all excavated burials were adult suggests that what was excavated at KKT in 2008 possibly represents part of a larger burial ground where age-related differential burial was practiced.

Table 1. Attributes of Sex Assessment.

OS COXAE		
	Male	**Female**
General attributes (Brothwell 1981: 62)	Massive, narrow and high	Gracile, broad and low
	Large muscle-attachments	Small muscle-attachments
Iliac Crest (During, pers. comm.)	Clear S-shape	Less clear S-shape
Os pubis (Bass 1987: 200–201)	Shorter	Longer
Subpubic angle (Brothwell 1981: 62)	Narrow	> 90°
Ventral Arc (Phenice 1969)	Not present	Present
Subpubic Concavity (Phenice 1969)	Lack of concavity	Concavity present
Ischiopubic Ramus Ridge (Phenice 1969)	Broad medial surface	Ridge on medial aspect
Arc Composé (Novotny 1982)	Single curve	Double curve
Preauricular sulcus (Buikstra and Ubelaker 1994: 18–19)	Faint or absent	Notable groove or depression
Greater Sciatic Notch (Buikstra and Ubelaker 1994: 18)	Narrow, U-shaped	Broad, V-shaped
Auricular surface (Bass 1987: 202)	Flat or somewhat concave	Raised
Foramen Obturatum (Bass 1987: 202)	Small and triangular-shaped	Larger and oval-shaped
Acetabulum (Bass 1987: 202)	Smaller	Larger

SACRUM		
	Male	**Female**
Lateral View (Brothwell 1981: 61)	Less prominent arc	More prominent arc
	4th segment deepest point in hollow	3rd segment deepest point in hollow

CRANIUM		
	Male	**Female**
General attributes	Massive, larger	Lighter, smaller
	Larger muscle-attachments	Smaller muscle-attachments
Facial skeleton	Larger and broader	Smaller and narrower
Foramen Magnum	Large	Small
Nuchal Crest	Marked bony ledge	Smooth occipital surface
Mastoid process (Buikstra and Ubelaker 1994)	Large	Small
Supraorbital Margin	Thick, rounded margin	Sharp border
Supraorbital Ridge	Well developed	Small
Glabella	Massive prominence	Minimal prominence
Mental eminence	Massive mental eminence	Little or no projection
Frontale	Sloping	Rounded, vertical
Orbita	Square	Rounded
Angulus mandibulae (Lateral View)	Sharp angle, visible muscle-attachments	Rounded angle, smooth surface
Angulus mandibulae (Frontal View)	Angled outwards	No angle
Frontal Sinuses (Buikstra and Ubelaker 1994)	Larger	Smaller

Catalog of Burials (for locations, see Color Plate 2.1)

by Jessica Kaiser, Afaf Wahba Abd-el-Salam, Brianne Daniels, and Sandra Koch

Burial 452 (Square 101.V28, Cut [21,882], Fill [29,453], Skeleton [29,454]), Color Plate 2.2

This burial was sunk into a poorly preserved mudbrick wall which has not yet been given a feature number. The skeletal remains were from an adult, based on bone size, although not much remains of the skeleton. There was no coffin. Because of the poor preservation (the taphonomic score was "o"), sex could not be determined. The burial was truncated—the cranium was missing, as were the pelvis and lower limbs. No teeth were found, and no pathologies noted. MNI analysis indicated one individual.

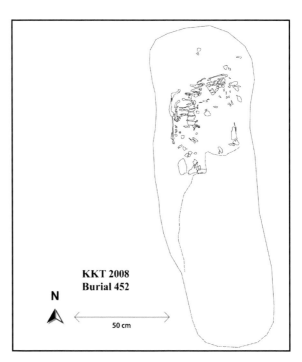

KKT 2008
Burial 452

N

50 cm

Figure 44. Burial 452, Skeleton [29,454].

Burial 453 (Square 101.U29, Cut [29,454], Fill [29,451], Skeleton [29,452]), Color Plate 3.1

Again, this burial was sunk into a poorly preserved mudbrick wall which has not yet been given a feature number. There was no coffin. The bones of this individual were eroded, indicating that they had been previously exposed. The taphonomic score was 0.05. However, enough remained to determine that this individual was a young male, aged approximately 16–21 years, but probably closer to 20. Age assessment was based on epiphyseal closure and non-closure, since no teeth were recovered. Sex assessment was based on the narrow sciatic notch. MNI analysis indicated one individual.

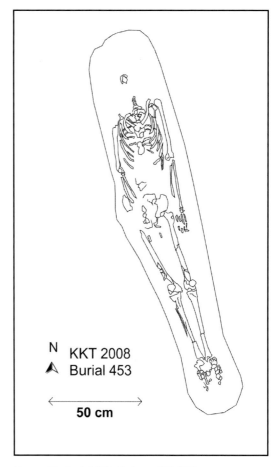

N KKT 2008
Burial 453

50 cm

Figure 45. Burial 453, Skeleton [29,452].

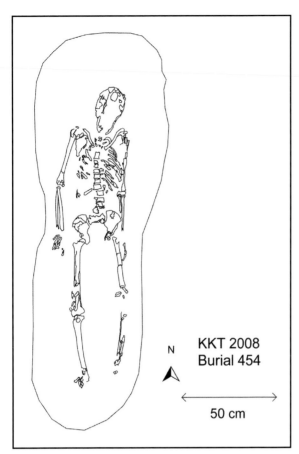

Figure 46. Burial 454, Skeleton [29,456].

Burial 454 (Square 101.U27, Cut [29,455], Fill [29,610], Skeleton [29,456], Coffin [29,457]), Color Plate 3.2

This burial was cut into an Old Kingdom mudbrick wall, which has not yet been given a feature number. Preservation was poor, with a taphonomic score of 0.04. Based on the wide sciatic notch and the severely worn teeth, the individual in the grave was assessed as an adult (Senilis) female, aged 50+. Pathologies noted were lipping on Thoracic vertebrae 11–12 and Lumbar 1 with a score of 2, according to Brothwell. The MNI analysis indicated one individual. In this burial, there were also traces of white pigment along the left side of the body, which possibly could be remnants of a coffin, although too little remained to be sure. Further, one tubular faïence bead was found in the fill of the burial.

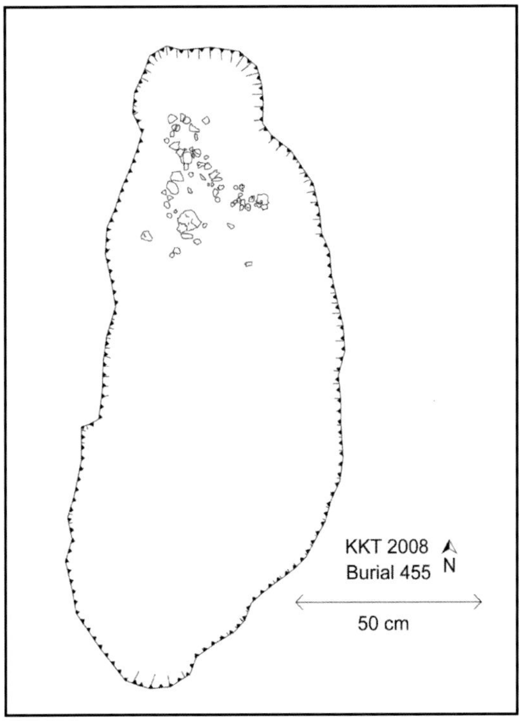

Figure 47. Burial 455, Skeleton [30,119].

Burial 455 (Square 101.T29, Cut [9,770], Fill [30,118], Skeleton [30,119]), Color Plate 4.1

This burial was cut into mudbrick wall [21,923] in Area KKT-F. The remains indicated that it was an older adult with severely worn teeth. There was no coffin. The burial had been truncated, most likely during the previous excavations of the area undertaken by Selim Hassan in the 1930s (Hassan 1943). The condition of the bone also indicated that the burial had been exposed for some time after the initial truncation. Due to the fragmented nature of the remains, the sex of the individual could not be determined. No pathologies were noted, also due to the lack of skeletal material that could be recovered, but one tubular faïence bead and some mother-of-pearl were recovered from the burial fill.

Burial 456 (Square 101.V30, Cut [29,960], Fill [29,961], Skeleton [29,968]), Color Plate 4.2

This burial was a shallow grave located on the edge of the Selim Hassan (1943) trench in Area KKT-F. It had been truncated by a robber's cut [29,962] which truncated the lower leg bones of the body and disturbed the grave. It may also have been truncated from above, most likely during the Hassan excavations. It was an adult burial, most likely female, judging from the mastoid process fragments. The bones were very fragmented and the only easily identifiable pieces belonged to the humerus. Some of the other pieces may belong to other long bones as well and will be studied further in the storeroom. No pathologies were noted and no teeth were recovered. In the robber's cut [29,962], secondary bones were found and those were designated as skeleton [29,965] in fill [29,963]. The fragmented pieces were from the left fibula and tibia, and since there were no duplicates, they most likely originally belonged to skeleton [29,968], but had been re-deposited.

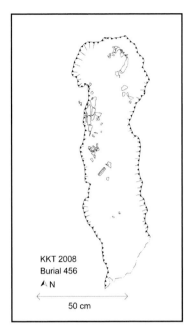

KKT 2008
Burial 456
N
50 cm

Figure 48. Burial 456, Skeleton [29,968].

Burial 457 (Square 101.V–W27–28, Cut [30,121], Fill [30,122], [30,123], [30,205]), Color Plate 5.1

This was a primary double burial, containing an older male [30,211] and a female [30,210]. The female skeleton was lying partially on her right side, loosely flexed, with her head on the thorax area of the male who was lying extended on his back. There was no indication of disturbance in the burial fills, so the two individuals appear to have been interred together. Further, judging from the burial positions, they were not tightly wrapped at the time of burial. The burial was covered by a pottery-rich deposit [30,122], overlying large limestone boulders [30,123] that weighed 412 kg, with one worked stone that weighed 35 kg. A limestone grinding stone was also recovered from the limestone feature. Underneath the limestone layer was a yellow sand fill, [30,205]. Also, one tubular faïence bead was recovered from the fill of Burial 457.

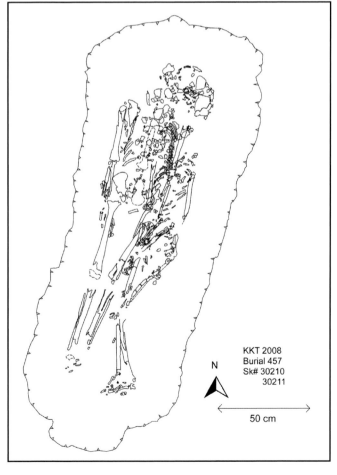

KKT 2008
Burial 457
Sk# 30210
30211
N
50 cm

Figure 49. Burial 457, Skeletons [30,210] and [30,211].

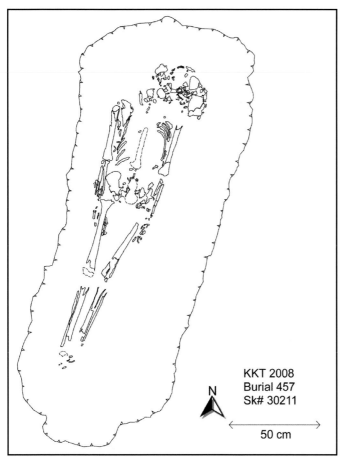

Figure 50. Burial 457, Skeleton [30,211].

Burial 457 (Square 101.V–W27–28, Cut [30,121], Fill [30,122], [30,123], [30,205], Skeleton [30,211]), Color Plate 5.1

This skeleton belonged to an older adult male. The age was based on the dental wear and degeneration of the joints and spine. The sex was determined from the large mastoid process, flaring angulus mandibulae, and narrow sciatic notch. We were able to take approximate lengths *in situ* for the long bones as the fragmented nature of the bones would not preserve that information for further analysis in the lab. The stature analysis indicated that this individual was quite tall, approximately 177.8 cm (or between 173.6 to 182 cm with error margins taken into account). Pathologies noted were eburnation on the TMJ and Atlas. Osteophytic growth was noted on the Atlas (temporo-mandibular joint) and Axis with a score of 3 according to Brothwell. A nonmetric trait noted was a split hypoglossal canal. Molar dental wear was between 5+ to 5++ according to Brothwell's, indicating an age over 45 years of age. Further, the uneven wear of the maxillary incisors and left premolars suggest that this individual may have been using his teeth as tools.

Burial 457 (Square 101.V–W27–28, Cut [30,121], Fill [30,122], [30,123], [30,205], Skeleton [30,210]), Color Plate 5.1

This individual was an older female. The age was based on dental wear which indicated advanced age, at least over 45 years of age according to Brothwell. Sex assessment was based on the wide sciatic notch, which was photographed *in situ*. Approximate measurements of some of the long bones were taken *in situ* as they were fragmented and measurements would not be possible after lifting. Several pathologies were noted: Cribra Orbitalia (healed), Occipital porosity (active), Porotic Hyperostosis on the left parietal (active), medium lipping of the Lumbar vertebrae (L4, L5), lipping of a thoracic vertebrae with a score of 1 according to Brothwell (the individual vertebra could not be determined), osteophytic growth on the left thumb metacarpal with a score of 1, and finally osteophytic growth with a score of 2 on one of the medial phalanges of the left hand. One sesamoid was also found in the left pedis.

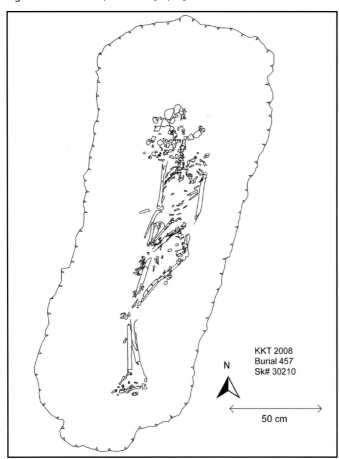

Figure 51. Burial 457, Skeleton [30,210].

Burial 458 (Square 101.S–T28, Cut [30,102], Fill [30,103], [30,120], Skeleton [30,202]), Color Plate 5.2

This burial was cut into wall feature [21,876] and covered by a layer of limestone [30,120] that together weighed 143 kg. It is possible that there originally was more limestone covering the burial, since the body below the limestone layer had quite clearly been disturbed at some point, and the stones re-deposited. The individual in the burial was an adult, but sex could not be determined due to the fact that most of the skeleton was missing. Age assessment was based on epiphysial fusion. The lower portion of the body was truncated and the skeletal remains were missing. In the area where the legs would have been there was more pottery than in the rest of the fill, possibly remnants of a separate robbery cut. However, this was not recognized during excavation, and the fill under the stones was taken out as one feature [30,103]. No cranial bones or dentition was recovered, and no pathologies noted.

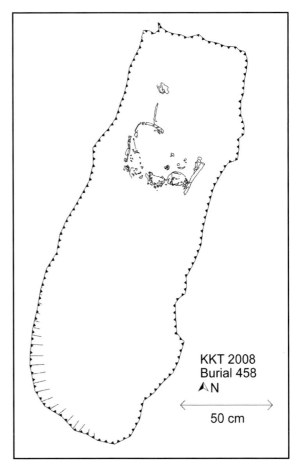

Figure 52. Burial 458, Skeleton [30,202].

Burial 459 (Square 101.U–V30, Cut [30,203], Fill [30,204], Skeleton [30,206]), Color Plate 6.1

This burial cut truncated two walls: wall [29,957] and wall [21,909]. The burial had been almost completely "scooped out," and only the lowest 2–3 cm of the bottom of the burial pit remained. This truncation most likely occurred during the Selim Hassan excavations in the 1930s. Of the skeleton, only a few fragments (~13) remained and no dentition was found. Determination of exact bone type of the fragments is awaiting final laboratory analysis. Age and sex assessment were impossible. No pathologies were noted.

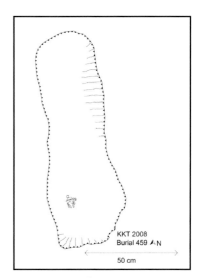

Figure 53. Burial 459, Skeleton [30,206].

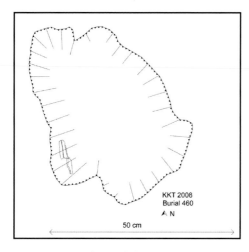

Figure 54. Burial 460, Skeleton [30,209].

Burial 460 (Square 101.V30, Cut [30,207], Fill [30,208], Skeleton [30,209]), Color Plate 6.2

This burial was cut by another feature previously excavated by Selim Hassan. Only a few fragments, most likely of a leg bone, were found. It was a shallow burial in a mudbrick wall with a limestone layer beneath the skeletal fragments. Due to the small amount of bone left, we were not able to determine the sex or age and no pathologies were noted.

Shown at twice the scale of others due to small size.

References

Acsádi, G., and J. Nemeskéri
1970   *History of Human Life Span and Mortality.* Budapest: Akadémiai Kiadó.

Aufderheide, A. C., and C. Rodriguez-Martin
1998   *The Cambridge Encyclopedia of Human Paleopathology.* New York: Cambridge University Press.

Bass, W. M.
1987   *Human Osteology: A Laboratory and Field Manual.* Third Edition. Columbia, MO: Missouri Archaeological Society.

Brooks, S., and J. M. Suchey
1990   Skeletal Age Determination Based on the Os Pubis: A Comparison of the Acsádi-Nemeskéri and Suchey-Brooks Methods. *Human Evolution* 5: 227–238.

Brothwell, D. H.
1981   *Digging Up Bones.* British Museum Publications. Oxford: Oxford University Press.

Buikstra, J. E., and D. H. Ubelaker (eds.)
1994   *Standards for Data Collection from Human Skeletal Remains.* Arkansas Archaeological Survey Research Series 44. Fayetteville, AR: Arkansas Archaeological Survey.

Cox, M.
2000   Ageing Adults from the Skeleton. In *Human Osteology in Archaeology and Forensic Science*, edited by M. Cox and S. Mays, 61–82. London: Greenwich Medical Media Ltd.

Gejvall, N.-G.
1960   *Westerhus: Medieval Population and Church in the Light of Skeletal Remains.* PhD, Lund University.

Hassan, S.
1943   *Excavations at Giza. Vol. IV. 1932–1933.* Cairo: Government Press.

Hodges, D. C.
1991   Temporomandibular Joint Osteoarthritis in a British Skeletal Population. *American Journal of Physical Anthropology* 85: 367–377.

Isçan, M. Y., S. R. Loth, and R. K. Wright
1984   Age Estimation from the Ribs by Phase Analysis: White Males. *Journal of Forensic Sciences* 29: 1094–1104.
1985   Age Estimation from the Ribs by Phase Analysis: White Females. *Journal of Forensic Sciences* 30: 853–863.

Ikram, S., and A. Dodson
1998   *The Mummy in Ancient Egypt: Equipping the Dead for Eternity.* London: Thames and Hudson.

Jit, I., V. Jhingan, and M. Kulkarni
1980   Sexing the Human Sternum. *American Journal of Physical Anthropology* 53: 217–224.

Krogman, M. W.
1962   *The Human Skeleton in Forensic Medicine.* Charles C. Thomas: Springfield, IL: Greenwich Medical Media Ltd.

Leek, F. F.

1972   Teeth and Bread in Ancient Egypt. *Journal of Egyptian Archaeology* 58: 126–132.

Lovejoy, C. O., R. S. Meindl, T. R. Pryzbeck, and R. P. Mensforth

1985   Chronological Metamorphosis of the Auricular Surface of the Ileum: A New Method for the Determination
            of Adult Skeletal Age at Death. *American Journal of Physical Anthropology* 68: 15.

Museum of London

1994   *Archaeological Site Manual.* London: MOLAS.

Nathan, H.

1962   Osteophytes of the Vertebral Column. *Journal of Bone Joint Surgery* 44A(2): 243–268.

Novotny, V.

1982   *Détermination du sexe du fragment fossile de l'os coxal gauche Arago*, Premiere Congres Internationale de
            Paleontologie Humaine XLIV. Niza, Spain.

Ortner, D. J., and W. G. J. Putschar

1985   *Identification of Pathological Conditions in Human Skeletal Remains.* Washington, DC: Smithsonian
            Institution Press.

Phenice, T. W.

1969   A Newly Developed Method of Sexing in the Os Pubis. *American Journal of Physical Anthropology* 30:
            297–301.

Roberts, C., and K. Manchester

1995   *The Archaeology of Disease.* Second Edition. New York: Cornell University Press.

Roksandic, M.

2002   Position of Skeletal Remains as Key to Understanding Mortuary Behavior. In *Advances in Forensic
            Taphonomy*, edited by W. D. Haglund and M. H. Sorg, 95–113. Boca Raton, FL: CRC Press.

Saunders, S. R.

1989   Non-Metric Variation. In *Reconstruction of Life from the Skeleton*, edited by M. Y. İşcan and K. A. R.
            Kennedy, 95–108. New York: Wiley-Liss, Inc.

Sjøvold, T.

1978   *Inference Concerning the Age Distribution of Skeletal Populations and Some Consequences for
            Paleodemography.* Antrop. Közl. 22: 99–114. Budapest: Akadémiai Kiadó.

Todd, T. W.

1920   Age Changes in the Pubic Bone: I. The White Male Pubis. *American Journal of Physical Anthropology* 3: 285.

1921   Age Changes in the Pubic Bone: II. The Pubis of the Male Negro-White Hybrid; III. The Pubis of the White
            Female; IV. The Pubis of the Female Negro-White Hybrid. *American Journal of Physical Anthropology* 4: 1.

Ubelaker, D. H.

1978   *Human Skeletal Remains: Excavation, Analysis, Interpretation.* Chicago, IL: Aldine Transaction Publishers.

White, T. D., and P. A. Folkens

2005   *The Human Bone Manual.* Burlington, MA: Elsevier-Academic Press.

Saqqara Laser Scanning Survey 2008

by Yukinori Kawae, Kosuke Sato, Hiroyuki Kamei, Tomoaki Nakano, and Ichiroh Kanaya

Introduction

In 2007 an Egyptian construction company under the supervision of Egypt's Supreme Council of Antiquities (SCA) began to restore both the interior and exterior of Egypt's oldest pyramid, the Step Pyramid at Saqqara, built around 2,700 BC for the 3rd Dynasty king with the Horus name Netjerykhet, more frequently called Djoser.

Prior to this restoration work, a French architect, Dr. Bruno Deslandes, carried out three-dimensional surveys and radar investigations of parts of the step pyramid. The restoration of monuments is necessary in site management, but subtle archaeological features can vanish with restoration. It is therefore imperative to record the present state of the monument in as detailed a manner as possible before any restoration work is carried out.

In 2006, Ancient Egypt Research Associates, led by Dr. Mark Lehner, collaborated with Tokyo Institute of Technology, Gangoji Institute, Osaka University, and Tohoku University of Art and Design to establish the Giza Laser Scanning Survey (GLSS). The team eventually produced a detailed three-dimensional model of the tomb of Queen Khentkawes [I] at Giza and also of the Worker's Cemetery located above AERA's HeG site.

Those projects prompted Dr. Zahi Hawass, the Secretary General of the SCA, to request the GLSS team

Figure 55. The Djoser Step Pyramid at Saqqara under the restoration work, northeast side. Photo by Yukinori Kawae. View to the southwest.

Giza Occasional Papers 4   63

take over Dr. Bruno's work for comprehensive three-dimensional documentation as quickly as possible before the restoration program was completed. For this purpose, the Saqqara Laser Scanning Survey (SLSS) team was formed largely from GLSS members, with the additional recruitment of three-dimensional laser specialists from DEVELO Solutions of Osaka, Japan.

Previous archaeological work on the survey area was mainly undertaken by Cecil M. Firth and James E. Quibell with Jean-Phillippe Lauer, who comprehensively studied and restored the Step Pyramid complex for more than 70 years.[1] According to Lauer, ancient builders started with a *mastaba* that they enlarged twice, beginning with a four-step pyramid that was raised to the final six-step version. Their works are indisputably seen as seminal studies on the foundations of pyramids. However, Lauer's theories are based on his own stylized plans and sections, which do not present the actual state of the monument. The aim of the SLSS was to produce a detailed three-dimensional model of the Step Pyramid as it really is today.

From May 25 to July 19, 2008, the SLSS team investigated the Step Pyramid using two types of unique laser scanners: the "Zoser Scanner," a custom-designed portable scanner developed by DEVELO Solutions, and two of Topcon's latest GLS-1000 laser scanners. This joint SCA-American-Japanese project produced a three-dimensional map of every millimeter of the Step Pyramid.[2]

Season's Objectives

One of the aims of the SLSS in 2008 was to produce a three-dimensional model composed of "point-clouds." In laser scanning, as the light beam sweeps over any surface it "captures" many thousands of points per second, each located to x, y, and z coordinates. A built-in or external digital camera records additional RGB color information. The point-cloud image of an ancient structure, such as the Step Pyramid, is itself an act of conservation, because it is, like all archaeological records (scale drawings, photographs, and field notes), an abstraction that represents the actual state at the time of the survey.

Unlike traditional "interpreted" line drawings, the three-dimensional data are minimally interpreted "raw" data, which is a basis for versatile exploitation in post-pro-

cessing: producing detailed three-dimensional representations and orthophotographs for two-dimensional drawings, recording the current restorations, and allowing the monitoring of long-term deterioration of the pyramid.

2008 Goals:

- Production of a detailed three-dimensional model of the exterior of the Step Pyramid for use as multi-purpose raw data.

- Acquisition of orthophotographs of a plan and sections of the pyramid, with images being printed at a 1:100 size of the monument at 350 dpi (20,000 × 10,000 pixels).

- Positioning of the exact location of the structure in terms of the Universal Transverse Mercator (UTM) coordinate system.

- Production of a three-dimensional movie (1280 × 720 pixels, 30 ftp).

Methodology

We applied two types of laser scanning systems to the Step Pyramid. A team from Topcon, Katsunori Tomita and Kazuto Otani, employed conventional ground-fixed laser scanners, Topcon GLS-1000, for basic, overall coverage of the pyramid. However, when we scan the pyramid from the ground with the commercially available scanners, the laser beams do not reach the top sides of the stones, and when we scan from above, they miss the underside of overhanging masonry, and so each course is left partly in shadow. To avoid such unscanned areas (shadow), Takaharu Tomii, CEO of DEVELO Solutions Inc., designed and manufactured the Zoser Scanner, which is a portable multiple scanner system, simultaneously producing laser beams that even reach behind small protuberances. With this method, while surveyors scan and move at a constant speed with the scanner, accurate information for the position and the attitude of the scanner are gained by an automatic target tracking total station with an inertial navigation system (gyroscope).

The Zoser Scanner was carried on the backs of professional climbers, Yoshihiko Yamamoto and Risei Sato, as they rappelled down the faces of each of the six gigantic steps of the pyramid. Four miniature scanners, two on each wing, projected infrared signals that brushed the pyramid fabric and gathered coordinates and elevations at the exceedingly fast rate of 40,000 points per second. A 1/2-inch CCD digital camera accompanied each of the four miniature scanners. The four cameras mounted on the Zoser Scanner took 68,000 close-up photographs of the pyramid fabric. The scanner looked like a giant dragonfly alighting on the pyramid.

1. Firth, C. M., J. E. Quibell, and J.-P. Lauer. 1935. *The Step Pyramid*. Fouilles à Saqqarah. Cairo: Institut Français d'Archéologie Orientale.

—Lauer, J.-P., and P. Lacau. 1936. Le pyramide à degrés, l'architecture, Fouilles à Saqqarah. Cairo: Institut Français d'Archéologie Orientale.

2. Our team would like to thank Mr. Kosuke Ueyama (CEO of TriAx Corp.) for his generous support of the SLSS 2008 season.

Figure 56. SLSS Federation logos on the body of the Zoser Scanner. The Egyptian Supreme Council of Antiquities; Ancient Egypt Research Associates Inc.; Osaka University; and DEVELO Solutions of Osaka, Japan. Photo by Yukinori Kawae.

Figure 57. Field Director Yukinori Kawae with the Topcon GLS-1000 fixed laser scanner. View to the northeast.

Figure 58. Yamamoto carries the Zoser Scanner on his back as he rappels down a face of the Step Pyramid. The Zoser Scanner laser-scans and photographs during the descent. Rappelling down the southern side. Photo by Yukinori Kawae.

Figure 59. Yamamoto with Zoser Scanner on his back. Photo by Yukinori Kawae. South face of the pyramid (southwest corner).

Equipment

The following equipment was used for positioning and three-dimensional modeling of the Step Pyramid:

Global Positioning System

Topcon GB-1000

Performance Specification:

(Note: the following are dependent on conditions; assume a quality GPS/LONASS constellation above 15° in elevation and operation of the receiver in adherence with procedures described in the TPS receiver operation manuals. In areas susceptible to high levels of multipath, during periods of high DOP, and during periods of ionospheric disturbance, performance may be degraded).

Static, Rapid Static	H: 3 mm + 0.5 ppm (x base line length)
	V: 5 mm + 0.5 ppm (x base line length)
RTK	H: 10 mm + 1 ppm
	V: 15 mm + 1 ppm

Laser Scanners

DEVELO Zoser Scanner-1

Inertial Navigation Unit	
Yaw	0.01 [deg]
Roll/Pitch	0.01 [deg]
Rate	100 [Hz]
Three-dimensional Scanner Unit	
Range of scanning	60 to 4095 [mm]
Angle of scanning	+/-120 [deg]
Resolution of scanning	0.36 [deg]
Scan rate	100 [ms]/line
Digital Camera Unit	
Imager	1/2-inch CCD interlace scanning
Resolution	1392 × 1040 [pix]
Size of pixel	4.65 × 4.65 [micrometer]
Lens mount	C mount

Topcon GLS-1000

System performance:

Maximum range at specified reflectivity	330 m at 90%, 150 m at 18%
Calculated range at 18%	150 m
Single Point Accuracy	
Distance	4 mm at 150 m
Angle (Vertical)	6"
Angle (Horizontal)	6"

Laser Scanning System:

Type	Pulsed
Color	Invisible (Eye Safe Laser)
Laser Class	Class 1
Scan Rate	3,000 points/second
Scan Density (Resolution)	
Spot Size	6 mm at 40 m
Maximum Sample Density	1 mm at 100 m
Field-of-view (Per Scan)	
Horizontal	360° (maximum)
Vertical	70° (maximum)
Color Digital Imaging	2.0 megapixel digital camera

Total Station

Leica TCRP 1205+

Angle measurement:

Accuracy (standard deviation, ISO 17123-3)

Hz, V 1	5" (1.5 mgon)
Display resolution	0.1" (0.1 mgon)

Method   absolute, continuous, diametrical

Compensator

Working range	4' (0.07 gon)
Setting accuracy	1.5" (0.5 mgon)
Method	Centralized dual axis compensator

Distance measurement (IR-Mode):

Range (average atmospheric conditions)

Round prism (GPR1)	3000 m
360° reflector (GRZ4)	1500 m
Mini prism (GMP101)	1200 m
Reflective tape (60 mm × 60 mm)	250 m
Shortest measurable distance	1.5 m

Accuracy/Measurement time (standard deviation, ISO 17123-4)

Standard mode	1 mm + 1.5 ppm/typ. 2.4 s
Fast mode	3 mm + 1.5 ppm/typ. 0.8 s
Tracking mode	3 mm + 1.5 ppm/typ. <0.15 s
Display resolution	0.1 mm
Method	Special phase shift analyzer (coaxial, visible red laser)

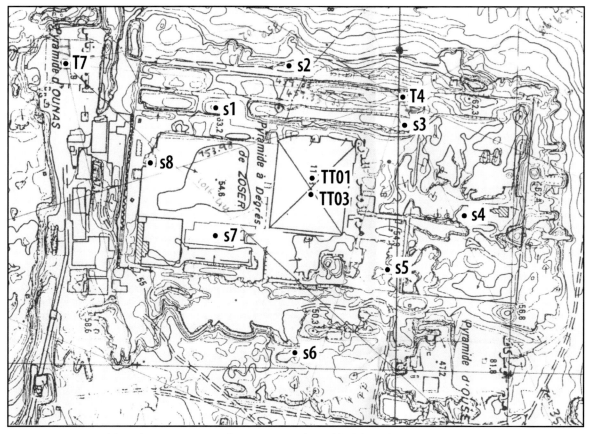

Figure 60. Position of the reference points on the Step Pyramid, modified from the MHR 1:5000 map series, 1978, sheet H 22.

Global Positioning Standard Points of the Site

Points T2, T4, and T7, whose coordinates had been given by David Jeffreys of University College London, were first chosen as a standard point for GPS of the SLSS.[3] Then, we marked 12 reference points on/around the pyramid (see figure 60 for approximate locations of the points). The two points, T4 and T7, were measured with GPS (Topcon GB-1000) in terms of the UTM36 coordinate system, and the other ten points were set up by traverse surveying with a total station (Leica TCRP 1205+). The accuracy of these point were within 4 mm horizontally and 19 mm vertically. Table 2 shows the coordinate values of the reference points.

3. We would like to thank David Jefferys for sharing his information on GIS values at Saqqara. Point T2 is on top of the pyramid of Teti, and therefore not on Figure 60.

Table 2. Coordinates of the Reference Points in UTM 36.

Reference point	X (m)	Y (m)	Ellipsoidal altitude (m)
S.1	795666.279	635664.391	79.589
S.2	795733.331	635633.793	79.445
S.3	795853.949	635679.071	79.357
S.4	795931.892	635789.934	72.425
S.5	795812.421	635850.527	79.809
S.6	795706.886	635962.658	71.623
S.7	795608.530	635826.215	76.819
S.8	795508.962	635739.925	73.409
T4	795846.794	635639.784	79.462
T7	795388.681	635606.739	89.336
TT01	795722.150	635760.848	130.348
TT03	795721.932	635772.333	130.224

Figure 61. One of 68,000 close-up photographs of pyramid fabric, limestone, and mortar, photographed by a 1/2-inch CCD digital camera on the Zoser Scanner.

Modeling

The custom-designed, portable Zoser Scanner (zs), was equipped with four DEVELO Scanning Range Finders, four 1/2-inch CCD digital cameras (C mount), a gyroscope, a target for the Leica TCRP 1205+, and a tablet PC.

The gyroscope of the zs measures its position, orientation, and velocity at the rate of 100 Hz (100 times per second). The four digital cameras accompanying each scanner took rapid sequence photographs of the pyramid fabric (fig. 61).

The body of the zs was automatically traced by the Leica TCRP 1205+ at the rate of 6-10 Hz, and the data was eventually synchronized by a GPS timer. The accuracy of the gyroscope depends on the number of satellites, and their orbits need to calibrate for at least half an hour after starting. Once it starts, the device should work with an uninterrupted power supply. If power is interrupted, the gyroscope needs to be re-calibrated. Therefore, the zs was connected to a long power cord during the survey to assure a continuous supply of electricity. The width of the zs wings is 2.5 m each. This required that the climbers, Yamamoto and Sato, rappel each face about 25 times (the monument is 109.02 m north-south × 121 m east-west × 58.63 m high).

The scanning of the whole pyramid with the zs was theoretically supposed to be completed within 14 days, but some practical difficulties, such as slow descending speed due to deterioration of the stones and the requirement of an uninterrupted power supply, required us to modify the original plan. But overall, the entire coverage of the pyramid was completed with the Topcon GLS-1000 scanning at the rate of 5 mm mesh from 35 different positions. The top of the pyramid, the four corner ridges, and one area at the southern side of the southern bottom step remained the only "shadow" areas, not covered by our scanning. Those data were integrated during post-processing.

Rendering/Data Processing

All the scanned data of GLS-1000 were integrated into a single point-cloud model on a computer at the head-quarters of Topcon in Tokyo. Topcon's original software, ScanMaster, generated point-cloud representations during post-processing. Color information from digital photographs taken by the built-in cameras on the scanner complemented 500 million points. We also used photos from a conventional hand-held digital camera to supplement color information.

After this process, Tomii created a three-dimensional movie (1280 × 720 pixels, 30 ftp) and orthophotographs (3,000 pixels) of a plan and sections of the pyramid. However, due to the excessive quantity of data, it was not feasible to export 20,000 pixel orthophotographic images of the Step Pyramid with Pointools. So, Dr. Kosuke Sato and Dr. Ichiroh Kanaya developed a special program which can generate large size orthophotographic images from the point-cloud data.

Results

Our original aim was to create an image of the Step Pyramid as it really is rather than an interpreted line drawing. An extensive three-dimensional point-cloud model of the exterior of the pyramid was mainly produced by Topcon GLS-1000(s), but supplemented by the custom creation and implementation of the Zoser Scanner. We produced a plan, and four cardinal elevations of the pyramid, all of which can be printed out in a 1:100 size of the monument at 350 dpi (see Color Plates 7 and 8).

Figure 62. The 2008 Saqqara Laser Scanning Survey team.

The 2008 AERA Team

PRESIDENT AND TREASURER
Dr. Mark Lehner

SENIOR STAFF
John Nolan, *Chief Financial Officer, Associate Director, Egyptologist*
Richard Redding, *Chief Research Officer, Archaeozoologist*
Mohsen Kamel, *Co-Field Director*
Ana Tavares, *Co-Field Director*
Mary Anne Murray, *Director of Archaeological Science,*
   Archaeobotanist
Erin Nell, *Business Manager*
Mari Rygh, *Archivist*
Brian Hunt, *Website Manager*
Farrah Brown, *GIS Manager*
Wilma Wetterstrom, *Science Editor*

GIZA: KHENTKAWES TOWN TEAM
2008 Excavations Team
Noha Bolbol, *SCA (Supreme Council of Antiquities)*
Pieter Collet
Delphine Driaux
Amelia Fairman
Mike House
Daniel Jones
Mark Lehner
Andrea Nevistic
Kasia Olchowska
Ana Tavares
Amanda Watts
Kelly Wilcox
Hassan Mohamed Ramadan, *SCA Trainee*
Gaber Abdel Dayem, *SCA Inspector for KKT excavations*
Nagla Hafez, *SCA Inspector for KKT excavations*

2008 Remote Sensing Team
Glen and Joan Dash
Richard Kosowsky

2008 Osteoarchaeology Team
Jessica Kaiser
Johnny Karlsson
Afaf Wahba, *SCA*
Ahmed Gabr, *SCA*
Amanda Agnew
Brianne Daniels
Sandra Koch
Sara Hassan Maraie, *SCA Trainee*

2008 ARCHAEOLOGICAL SCIENCE TEAM
Anna Wodzińska, *Ceramicist, Team Leader*
Edyta Klimaszewska, *Ceramicist*
Sherif Mohamed Abd el-Monaem, *Ceramicist, SCA*
Mohamed Aly Abd el-Hakiem Ismail, *Ceramicist, SCA*
Katarzyna Danys, *Ceramicist*
Karolina Gorka, *Ceramicist*
Sylwia Gromadzka, *Ceramicist*
Aleksandra Ksiezak, *Ceramicist*
Jessica Kaiser, *Osteologist, Team Leader*
Johnny Karlsson, *Osteologist*
Afaf Wahba, *Osteologist, SCA*
Ahmed Gabr, *Osteologist, SCA*
Amanda Agnew, *Osteologist*
Brianne Daniels, *Osteologist*
Sandra Koch, *Osteologist*
Sara Hassan Maraie, *Osteologist, SCA Trainee*
Mary Anne Murray, *Director of Archaeological Science and Giza*
   Field Lab, Archaeobotanist, Team Leader

Menna Allah el-Dorry, *Archaeobotanist*
Claire Malleson, *Archaeobotanist*
John Nolan, *Mud Sealings Specialist, Team Leader*
Richard Redding, *Archaeozoologist, Team Leader*
Kelly Wilcox, *Archaeozoologist*
Izumi Nakai, *XRD/XRF Specialist, Team Leader*
Kyoko Yamahana, *XRD/XRF Specialist*
Abe Yoshinari, *XRD/XRF Specialist*
Kriengkamol Tantrakarn, *XRD/XRF Specialist*
Ana Tavares, *Objects Specialist, Team Leader*
Emmy Malek, *Objects team*
Hanan Mahmoud Mohamed Mahmoud, *Objects team, SCA Inspector*
Ahmed Ezz, *Objects team, SCA Inspector*
Laurel Flentye, *Pigment Specialist*
Rainer Gerisch, *Wood charcoal Specialist*
Marina Milić, *Lithics Specialist*
Ashraf Abd el-Aziz, *Mudbrick Specialist*
Paul Nicholson, *Ceramics/Faience Specialist*
Yukinori Kawae, *Lab Photographer*
Jason Quinlan, *Lab Photographer, Videographer*

2008 GIS TEAM
Farrah Brown LaPan
Camilla Mazzucato
Rebekah Miracle
Shaimaa Fouad

2008 GIZA ARCHIVES TEAM
Mari Rygh, *Archivist*
Manami Yahata, *Data Entry*
Maha Ahmed Haseeb, *Office Assistant*
Fayrouz Ahmed, *Office Assistant*

2008 GIZA IT TEAM
Ahmed Basoumi
Jack Tavares
Mohamed Said

2008 SAQQARA LASER SCANNING SURVEY TEAM
Zahi Hawass, *(Secretary General, SCA), Director*
Mark Lehner, *Co-Director*
Kosuke Sato, *(Osaka University) 3-D Team Leader*
Hiroyuki Kamei, *(Professor, Tokyo Institute of Technology) Sub-Leader*
Tomoaki Nakano, *(Researcher, Ancient Orient Museum) Sub-Leader*
Yukinori Kawae, *(AERA) Laser Scanning Project Field Director*
Afif Roheim, *Chief Inspector, SCA*
Ichiroh Kanaya, *(Associate Professor, Osaka University) Visualization*
   Team Leader
Takaharu Tomii, *(CEO, DEVELO Solutions) 3-D Specialist*
Toshikazu Kameoka, *(DEVELO Solutions) 3-D Specialist*
Manami Yahata, *(AERA) Archaeological Documentation/Archive*
Yoshihiko Yamamoto, *Natural Consultant, Professional Climber*
Risei Sato, *Natural Consultant, Professional Climber*
Katsunori Tomita, *(Topcon) Laser Scanning Expert*
Kazuto Otani, *(Topcon) Laser Scanning Expert*

2008 BOSTON OFFICE TEAM
Aparna Das, *Archival Assistant*
Jim Schnare, *Associate Communications Manager*
Alexandra Witsell, *Assistant Editor, Sealings Assistant*

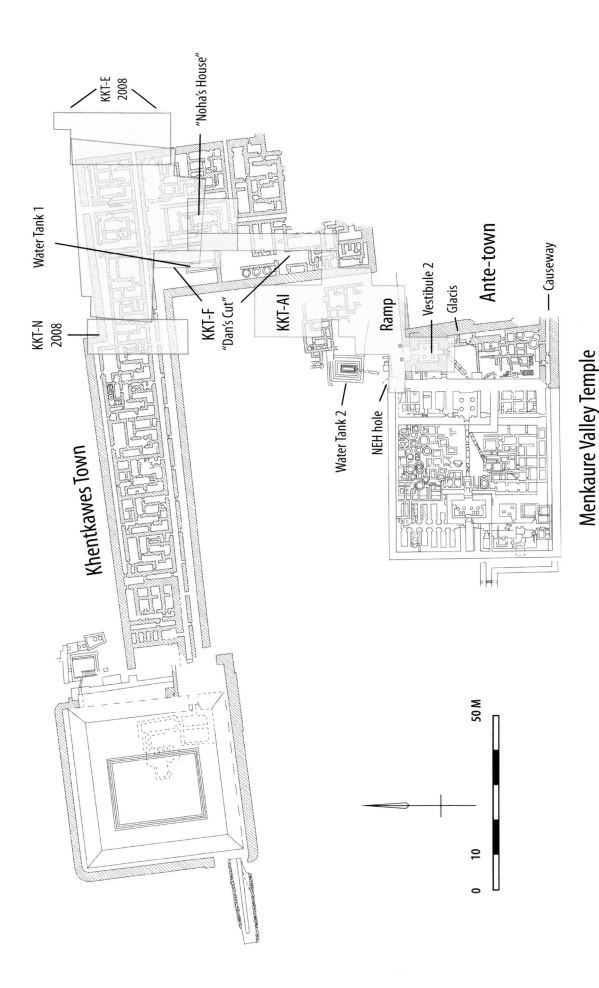

Color Plate 1.1. Area map of the Khentkawes monument, town (KKT), Menkaure Valley Temple (GIII.VT), and Ante-town, based on Selim Hassan's original map published in 1943. Yellow shading represents 2006-2007 GPMP excavations, blue is 2008.

Khentkawes Town

KKT-N 2008

Water Tank 1

KKT-E 2008

"Noha's House"

KKT-F "Dan's Cut"

KKT-AI

Ramp

Water Tank 2

NEH hole

Vestibule 2

Glacis

Ante-town

Causeway

Menkaure Valley Temple

0   10   50 M

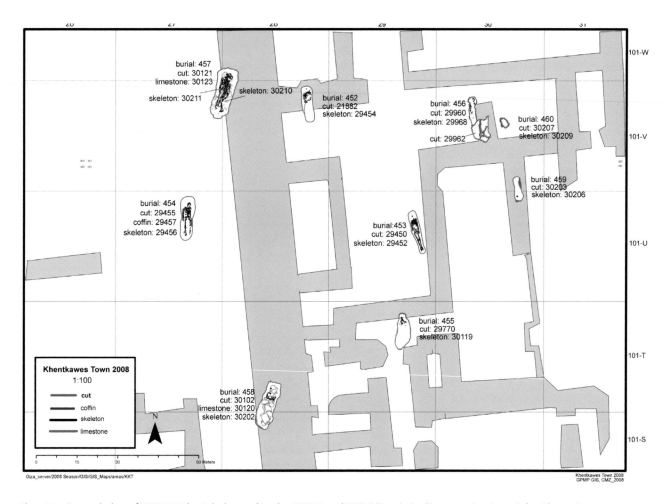

Plate 2.1. General plan of KKT 2008 burials, located in the KKT-AI and KKT-F "Dan's Cut" intersection (see Color Plate 1.1).

Plate 2.2. KKT, Burial 452. Photo by Johnny Karlsson.

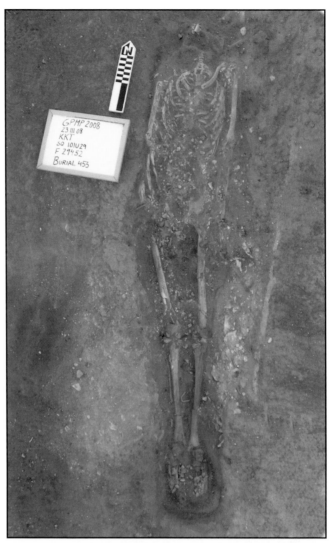

Plate 3.1. KKT, Burial 453. Photo by Johnny Karlsson.

Plate 3.2. KKT, Burial 454. Photo by Johnny Karlsson.

Plate 4.1. KKT, Burial 455. Photo by Jessica Kaiser.

Plate 4.2. KKT, Burial 456. Photo by Jessica Kaiser.

Plate 5.1. KKT, Burial 457. Photo by Jessica Kaiser.

Plate 5.2. KKT, Burial 458. Photo by Sandra Koch.

Plate 6.1. KKT, Burial 459. Photo by Sandra Koch.

Plate 6.2. KKT, Burial 460. Photo by Sandra Koch.

Plate 7.1. Preliminary version of the point cloud model of the Djoser Step Pyramid produced by GLS-1000. View of the southwest corner, looking northeast. Gaps remain until data from the Zoser Scanner are fully incorporated.

Plate 7.2. Preliminary version of the point cloud model of the Djoser Step Pyramid produced by GLS-1000. Eastern side of the pyramid. Gaps remain until data from the Zoser Scanner are fully incorporated.

Plate 8.1. Preliminary version of the point cloud model of the Djoser Step Pyramid produced by GLS-1000. Southern side of the pyramid. Gaps remain until data from the Zoser Scanner are fully incorporated.

Plate 8.2. Preliminary version of the point cloud model of the Djoser Step Pyramid produced by GLS-1000. Northern side of the pyramid. Gaps remain until data from the Zoser Scanner are fully incorporated.